THE NEAR-DEATH EXPERIENCE

Mysticism or Madness

THE NEAR-DEATH EXPERIENCE

Mysticism or Madness

By Judith Cressy

Founded 1910
THE CHRISTOPHER PUBLISHING HOUSE
HANOVER, MASSACHUSETTS 02339

Table of Contents

INTRODUCTION

I have been near death twice. In 1969 our middle daughter, Elspeth, died of leukemia. I was thirty-three and emotionally and philosophically unprepared for death. Eight years later, all the unshed tears burst the dam of my defenses, and I cried until I became unconscious. During the three days that I was "out," I had a mystical experience similar to those reported by people who have died and returned to life. Unlike that near-death experience (NDE) I did not experience leaving my body, travelling down a dark tunnel, entering heaven or encountering the Light. I travelled, as a Sufi teacher listening to my story later told me, into the Void, the domain of dark and imageless divinity. Upon return, I experienced many of the changes, called aftereffects, that accompany an NDE, and some of the same problems the near-death experiencer (NDEr) encounters on return to life. For instance, I acquired new energy, insight and information that were confusing until I understood what they were — the expected side effects of mystical experience. My family simply assumed I was crazy.

Mysticism or Madness is then a product of my mystical experience, personal pain and professional training. The year after my first mystical experience, I entered a mainline Protestant seminary. Busy being a mother, I graduated five years later and was ordained. For the next four years I served as pastor to a small country church. The experience that I had buried for nine years began, however, to knock insistently on the door of my psyche when NDEr Tom Sawyer identified me as "one of the family." I was forced to recognize that something wonderful and fearful had happened to me. Then the need to talk about and integrate that event became as important to me as to other NDErs.

I quit my pastoral post and returned to seminary for doctoral studies in theology and pastoral counseling. The research for this book began with my work for the Doctor of Ministry thesis requirement. My purpose then, as now, is to make certain that NDErs receive the compassionate personal and professional treatment they deserve as they struggle to return to life from the brink of death.

The real pain of reentry into life, or recovery from death, has been disguised by the wonder and glory of the NDE. It is time to balance the near-death picture. These people attain their spiritual treasure by a painful death and a difficult recovery.

In *Mysticism or Madness*, I have collected the data of near-death recovery from scattered sources, mostly journal articles, and added my own insights and observations, especially on the aspect of near-death recovery called "spiritual crisis." I have, however, focused on the most damaging impediment to good recovery: the label of "craziness" by family and friends, and the diagnosis of psychosis by professionals. NDErs are often alienated from their families for this reason and thrown into psychiatric institutions by professionals who believe they are mad.

Two definitions of insanity work against the NDEr — the cultural and the clinical. In the chapter on mysticism I counter the cultural argument by making a case for the NDE as mystical experience, and presenting a defense of the mystical world-view. In the chapter on near-death recovery, I address the clinical dimension by attempting a distinction between psychotic symptoms and near-death look-alikes. I believe that a good differentiation is only possible after personal experience with both psychotics and NDErs. A year as counselor under supervision at the Rochester Psychiatric Center and two years as co-founder and co-facilitator of the Rochester, New York, near-death support group have given me that experience.

I feel, however, that the context for clinical assessment has to be shifted from the medical model to a spiritual one in order for the NDEr to receive adequate treatment. When the medical model is laid over the near-death experiencer, the changes in them that are truly spiritual look crazy, and their real needs are either ignored or go undetected. Therefore the work of transpersonal psychology, that branch of psychology that trains practitioners in both spiritual and clinical disciplines, seemed appropriate, particularly the theoretical insights of Ken Wilber and the concept of spiritual crisis developed by Christina and Stanislov Grof.

Is the NDE, however, truly spiritual? To make a case for that I compare the NDE and its aftereffects (those transforming and troubling changes that accompany an NDE) to the experiences and accompanying changes of two great Christian mystics, St. Theresa of Avila and St. John of the Cross. I chose them because I am a Christian and because my initial work was conducted in a Christian seminary. However, I also believe the inclusion of Christian mysticism may be important to many people. Though we live in a post-Christian era, we still exist in a Christian culture — one created by and permeated with Christian images and ideas. Knowledge that an experience like theirs exists in the history of their own tradition may help many NDErs to become reconciled to their religious or cultural roots.

I do not confine myself, however, to Christianity, but compare the phases of the NDE (leaving the body, travelling through a dark tunnel, entering heaven, or encountering the Light) to the universal stages of mystical consciousness identified by Ken Wilber. Conclusions from this endeavor also help to balance the near-death picture. Through the comparison to the mystical experiences of John and Theresa, the depth of the near-death mystical experience is apparent. Comparison to the stages and standards of the world's spiritual traditions, saints and sages, shows them to be less than perfect. *NDErs are neither saints, nor insane. They are becoming mystics, not going mad.*

To prepare the reader for the central chapters on mysticism and near-death recovery, I tell near-death stories in Chapters 1-3, and describe the near-death experience and its aftereffects in Chapters 4-5. In the first three chapters you will meet Howard, Grace and Dianne (not her real name.) They will tell you about their lives before the NDE, and speak to you in their own words about their experience and the difficulties of returning to life.

Though the stories, in general, conform to the near-death pattern, each is unique. Grace enters "heaven" and meets her Lord. After a "hellish" experience, Howard is lifted up toward a Being of Light and merges with lesser light entities. Dianne immediately enters a loving and beautiful blackness. In these stories, the reader has an opportunity to enter a profound and personal relationship with three NDErs: to understand what preceded their NDE and to be privy to the pain and problems of their recovery. These three personalize and complement the short anecdotal sketches used throughout the book to illustrate my arguments. In the intensely personal and private domain of spiritual experience, first person narrative may be the best, if not the only method of assessment. I find the compilation of many, many first-person narratives convincing.

Throughout the book I adopt a tone of acceptance of the NDE. After all, I have had one, and could not be expected to be a skeptic concerning the reality and validity of the experience. As a trained professional, on the other hand, I do not need to accept every aspect of the NDE at face value. Nor have I. Having carefully researched, observed and pondered, I have come to the conclusions reached in this book — that the NDEr is neither a saint nor insane; not mad, but a mystic who nevertheless may require professional care, and, at the very least, the sympathy of family, friends and society. The objective of the book, which is to present a more balanced picture of the NDE than usual, is, I believe, written in a balanced voice — one that is neither wholly personal nor wholly professional. Consequently I can speak in two directions — to the NDEr, family and friends for whom this information may be helpful; and to helping professionals: psychoanalysts, pastors, doctors, nurses and others who may encounter a NDEr in their practice. I speak also to the serious spiritual seeker as well as the skeptic.

In *Mysticism or Madness* I do not address all the questions raised by the NDE. In particular, I do not talk specifically about death, though, God knows! our culture needs new positive images to replace old inadequate or negative ideas. This is a book then about the living and for the living. It is about those who have returned to life, not left for good. It is for them and for us, to remind us of the great issues of life and death, and assuage our hunger for spiritual experiences.

To render the book readable, I have eliminated footnotes. Primary sources for the near-death experience and aftereffects are Kenneth Ring, *Life at Death* and *Heading Toward Omega*; Margot Grey, *Return from Death*; Raymond Moody, *Life After Life*; and Carol Zalesky, *Otherworld Journeys*. For the chapter on mysticism, the primary sources are *The Collected Works of St. John of the Cross, The Life of Teresa of Jesus* and *Interior Castle of Teresa of Avila*. These and other cited sources are listed in the bibliography. I acknowledge my indebtedness to all researchers in near-death studies, mysticism and counseling, without whom my work would have been impossible; and to all my family, friends, editors, typists who put up with me, and worked unceasingly for little reward. I am, however, especially grateful to the NDErs who have been courageous enough to defy cultural convention and share their stories, particularly Dianne, Grace, and Howard.

I would like, however, to conclude with a personal confession. While I believe it is important that each NDEr return to full life and health, I don't believe that either the experience or their recovery is an isolated event. I believe we stand poised at an historic turning point. Like the NDEr who returns with a prophetic vision, I believe we are likely to encounter some form of global catastrophe. And when it is finished, humanity will again have the opportunity to recreate the world as it was meant to be — a Paradise of love and peace.

The NDEr has an important role to play in this. They have been given an opportunity to return to life to tell the rest of us what death is like, but also to prepare us for the eventuality of global crisis and recovery. They are messengers of hope and models for the earth in her own potential near-death experience.

Chapter 1
Dianne

Dianne and I sit in the kitchen of her comfortable cape. The odor of cream of broccoli soup mingles with the warmth of family life. A son is home from college, and her husband from work. Soon another son and daughter will arrive from high school. Dianne divides her attention between them and our discussion. She is anxious. It has only been two years since the meningitis responsible for her death, and she still finds it difficult to talk about her NDE.

Dianne finds it easier to talk about her early life. She begins with early memories that, like Grace's, appear arbitrary, but have a bearing on the meaning of the NDE.

> DIANNE: I remember when I was about eight or nine years old, standing in front of my house looking up at the sky and seeing all the stars and saying when I grew up that I wanted to be the type of person who studies the stars, to find out what they are, why they're there, what they do. At that time, that was a long time ago, that person was called a scientist. I still remember that like it was yesterday.

That moment marked the end of her childhood and the beginning of family abuse. It was the last faint flicker of the self she was supposed to become before her life became sheer survival — a self she is recovering since her NDE.

> DIANNE: The childhood was not that great, so when I got into high school it was more of an escape from the family life. I was able to escape the family and withdraw into my friends. That was easier than having to go home. I graduated from high school in June and got married in July, which was a very good way to escape the family. I think what was calling was the animalistic instinct to get away from the harm that was being caused at home. It was very abusive.
>
> So, yeh, I left. I was probably about sixteen when I first met Scott. He was over to the house one day. My father had gotten very angry with me. My knight in shining armor came up, grabbed my father by the shirt tails and said, "If you ever lay a hand on her again, I'll kill you." And of course, my father never laid a hand on me again. Scott became the man who was going to save me from the physically abusive father. It was a great escape for me to be able to withdraw into Scott and get away. I know I was young.

1

I probably shouldn't have gotten married so young — young to have children, young to have the responsibility.

About the time she met Scott, Dianne contracted lupus. Daily life became increasingly painful, and by the time of her NDE Dianne rarely left her house.

DIANNE: Prior to the NDE, I was in a very depressed state and didn't even know it. I was having a lot of pain, and I was working. I was taking care of four little toddlers. I suppose that was self-punishment, that I thought I needed to take care of four toddlers, plus the house, plus my own three children.

And every day they would come, and every day I would work taking care of those poor little kids. And every night I'd get into bed in tremendous pain, with every joint in the body, every joint swollen up. I remember crawling into bed and asking God, "Please don't make another day to come. I don't want to wake up tomorrow morning. This is too much for me to handle. I can't take another day of work." It had become work to me. Life had become work.

So that went on for seven or eight months. The morning I first got sick, it was, uh, I remember the children coming in. I can picture this as if I was watching a movie going on. It's very bizarre. That still stays with me, the actual onset of the meningitis.

It was more than the body being sick. There was something strange going on inside the body. I remember making a cup of tea and all of a sudden the whole entire body had this rush. I remember screaming out my son's name, and running over to the couch cause I was going to fall down. I remember saying to Jerry when he came over to the couch, "I don't know what's the matter with me. But all of a sudden I feel very, very hot, like I'm boiling." Then I must have passed out or something.

And the very next thing I remember is being in the bed. He had put me in bed, and I remember being freezing cold, freezing cold. I have no idea where I was, who was there. The house was very, very strange. The house was gone and just me and the room. Nothing existed in the whole world except me and this room. And then they got me out of bed and got me dressed and took me to the doctor later that afternoon.

To me they were just moments. I would be unconscious between these moments. I remember being in the doctor's office, and fainting in the office. I remember entering his little room, laying on the bed and him telling me I had a very bad case of the flu. The reason I was reacting so bad was because I had lupus and that was just making it worse. He told me to go home. He told me to quit smoking, which I did. Never had a cigarette since.

And then the next thing I knew I was standing in the kitchen and Scott or somebody was saying that I looked bad. Somehow the bacteria had settled in the wrist. The doctors say that if the bacteria hadn't settled in the wrist — which is what brought me to the hospital — I probably would have died. They kept saying you just have a very bad case of the flu.

As the bacteria travelled throughout the body, it settled, they feel, in three or four different spots. My hand swelled up so it was about four times normal size. The fingers were touching, they were so swollen, so so painful. I was standing in the kitchen and said to Skip you either cut off this hand, or take me into the back yard and shoot me. There was no way I was going to stand this pain that's happening inside this wrist.

He put me in the car. I don't remember entering, but I remember being in the car and driving off. I don't remember anything after that. I remember being in the hospital. I don't know what was going on, but I suppose the closer I got to actually leaving the body completely, the room I was in was becoming smaller and smaller and I was becoming larger and larger.

Dianne is describing her subjective impressions of a slow death. Though there is a moment in the hospital when she felt she left the body for good, Dianne feels her NDE is unique because she was already dying at the onset of the illness.

DIANNE: I became one with the bedroom. I couldn't go beyond the bedroom. That was it. When I was in the kitchen, the kitchen was very, very small. The cupboards, the shelves and everything were very, very small, and I felt absolutely huge. The people were small. I would look at them and see them as these little tiny people. I must have been talking to them because they heard me.

And then when we were in the hospital, it was easier to fill the room. I couldn't fill the whole emergency room. I had this little space I was allowed to fill.

They took me some place at one time, and that bothered me a lot. When I left the cubicle I was in, I quickly went back into the body. I remember the sense of being small and I didn't like the sense of being small again.

So then I went back into the room. I must have been unconscious not to remember what was going on. Then I can remember all of a sudden being larger, being above the room, looking down at Scott and seeing him with his arms folded in the corner. People were standing around doing something. I don't know what they were doing. Jibber, jabbering. They'd say, "Now, let's go."

I remember looking at Scott, and he just stood there totally perplexed, not knowing what to do. Then I didn't see Scott anymore, and I didn't see me laying there anymore. There was just total darkness. But it wasn't scary. It isn't that kind of black.

It was everywhere. It was all around me. It was inside me. It was above me. I suppose now that I think about it, I was part of the blackness. That's who I was.

And this being was on my left side. Like um, I don't know how to explain what the being was like. He was respectful; wanting to help me, but respecting who I was. Like trying to hold me up, as if I needed to be held up, though I didn't need to be held up in the sense that you would be held up by somebody if you were walking. And this being stood next to me with his head bowed, and just being reassuring that he was there.

I had the sense of knowing where I was going, but not knowing where I was going; walking and moving, but not moving. And then the blackness that was all around me, oh it was beautiful. It was a very beautiful blackness, more like velvet. If you were to say that black was beautiful, you would say it would be like a velvet touch. And it was smooth and loving and very familiar.

And then up ahead was an indentation in the blackness. It went down, but it didn't go down, because it was everywhere. I used to explain it like it was an Abyss. But it wasn't an abyss like on the earth, it was just another place in the blackness that went on forever. It was so black, and it was so real and true. It went on forever. I knew that if I went beyond that, there was something else there. I didn't know what ever else was there. Later I thought it may be the Light.

When I realized where I was, sensed where I was going, I was then told that everything I was doing was on the wrong path and that I was going to start over. It wasn't that what I was doing was incorrect. There was no right or wrong. "I'm not punishing you," he said. "You're not a bad person. It's just that it's not working."

I know I'd read people having NDEs having a whole life review. I don't remember having a whole life review, having any incidents put before me. It was, yes, everything you've done so far wasn't what you originally wanted to do. You just start over. So we thought you'd like to start over, so you're going this way, toward the indentation.

And then I became very angry. I remember screaming out "no" three times. It's as if the blackness absorbed the words "no." There was no echo. It was part of the blackness. It belonged to the blackness. The blackness looked as if it was a thousand feet away, and then right under my face. It looked like I could touch it. I reached out and couldn't touch it. I screamed out "no" three times. "I have to take care of my daughter. Nobody can raise her like I can."

Then I remember turning around. I remember it being my left shoulder because the being was on my left. But there were no shoulders, and yet you feel there were. It was as if you brought the memory of the body with you, and yet you saw the body lying on the bed. You weren't afraid that you didn't bring the body. Who I was was still me, the being who had left the body. Who I was was totally intact.

I realized at that moment that the body lying down on this bed never was me. Yet this body was the one that felt all the pain, and this body was the reason why I left. It intrigues me now. So after screaming out that I was the only one who could raise my daughter, and giving reassurance that this was what I wanted, what I'd asked for, I returned.

Dianne's reason for returning was ostensibly to care for her child. However, as she recalled looking over her shoulder at Scott, she began to cry. It made her sad to think that with a single choice, she would have been "gone from that place forever." She still has "unfinished business" with Scott, things neither have forgiven.

Scott has been a savior often, and a supportive spouse. Dianne says that without him she would not have survived. He was her lifeline in the hospital, caring for her there and at home. Dianne didn't have an overwhelming experience of love and still finds it difficult to give and receive. Scott finds it difficult to talk and express emotions freely. They still have much to learn and teach each other in this lifetime.

Dianne also thinks she returned for a purpose, and asks "the guys" daily to disclose it to her. Part of the process of return, for Dianne, has been the search for her purpose or mission in life.

Return for her has not been easy. She returned to a body wracked with pain. For the first six months she recalls she was very, very angry. Angry with God for leaving her in pain. Angry with everybody.

> DIANNE: When I was in the hospital I kept getting cards and flowers, and the nurses would come in and say, "Oh look, you got flowers." And I'd say, "Who cares, I don't want flowers, who are these people anyway?" I remember getting into arguments with the doctors. "I give you warning, if you don't let me out of here, I'm leaving tomorrow. I'm pulling your stinkin' I.V. out and I'm walking down the hall whether you want me to or not." "Oh, OK, OK," they'd say.
>
> So they did their best to get me out. I came home with a tremendous amount of anger built up. And I remember the person I was most angry with was God. He had totally deserted me, left me in this body that couldn't do anything, not knowing I had made the choice myself.

Dianne didn't realize until a year later, while discussing her NDE with a friend, that she had made the choice herself. It takes time and talking to process an NDE.

Dianne also remembers another incident with a star that illuminates the reason for her anger and her NDE. A star story marked the moment her child and self-hood ended. In the hospital she sees another star, and feels like an alien and stranger to this world. This moment, however, marks the beginning of Dianne's new life; her renewed self-discovery and her journey toward re-entry and recovery.

> DIANNE: I can remember being in this hospital room and I couldnt' move, being very upset. I can remember saying to Scott, I can picture my head moving up, but when I go to do it, my head won't move up. And that bothered me. He just smiled and didn't say anything. And that night when he left, I looked out the window and there was this one star. I remember

looking at that star, so angry at God and thinking, "You put me here. I've been screaming to you for help, and you haven't come, you haven't taken any of this pain away. You didn't make any of the loneliness in the room go away. I still feel as lonely as I did five minutes ago. I don't feel any better."

I can remember looking at that star and thinking that star was the only friend I had in the entire world. There was nobody else that cared for me. There was nobody I cared for except this star. And then falling asleep with the star.

Dianne, like others who have left this world for another, feels like an alien on return. Dianne expressed the dislocation of living between worlds, the discomfort of the dark night of the soul, in anger. When she got home, she says:

DIANNE: If I had the keys, I'd just take the car and go out. If not I'd yell and scream, and run down the street, and then sit down and ask God, "What am I doing here? I don't belong here. I don't belong to this house, I don't belong to these kids. I don't know who they are. I don't know who this man is. I don't know what he wants of me. I don't know what the kids want of me."

I didn't see any of my family the way I used to. My aunts, cousins, sisters, nobody is the same to me anymore. Even my children, they've all changed. It was as if I had bonded with these people, and the bonding had come undone.

I never allowed myself to bond with my father, aunts, cousins, sister, brothers this time. And the bonding was very difficult between Scott and the children. It was very difficult. They thought they still had the bonding with me. Mine was gone. I didn't know who these people were. I'd look at these people and think, "Why are they taking care of me like this, why do they love me? What is it?" I remember looking at them. I remember being pregnant with this one, giving birth to that one. But what was the feeling? What was it? The feeling was gone.

Ties to this world, including emotional ones, are severed during an NDE. Dianne was realistically cautious about rebonding to family members who had or would abuse her. What had gone awry in her early life was being righted. Dianne says she feels that she belongs to the groups she has chosen since her NDE. Dianne is discovering her people and herself.

DIANNE: I had this tremendous urge to just read and read. Everybody stayed out of my way. They weren't allowed to bother me. I put aside three to six hours. I mean I would do the wash and the vacuuming. And if I didn't want to make supper, if I was into something: "Hey, you guys, that's tough," you know? I did my work this morning. You got what you wanted from me. Now just leave me alone. And that's how I looked at it. This [reading] was my job. And I did that for about a year.

Just a week or so ago I had an argument with my sister. She called Scott up and said: "I think there's something wrong with Dianne. She talks about all these weird and bizarre things. Doesn't she realize the books she's reading are just for entertainment? Those things aren't real." I was reading about Buddhism and Hinduism, different philosophies on life, different religions. I thought it was absolutely fabulous. And I may have picked up a couple of books on healing. I did. I had taken one course on healing with someone out of New York City. And she talked of healing through the chakras. So all this fit in, you know. The chakras were part of the Hindu religion. This whole thing was fabulous. When I heard my sister it really scared me. I had no idea anybody would sit there and say, you know, I think you're crazy for what you think. You should be locked up.

Dianne's brother also called her crazy. He told her that things like that only happened in books by people like Raymond Moody, but not to her. Ignorant remarks like these are upsetting, and retard recovery. Despite their objections, however, Dianne continued to read and began to philosophize.

DIANNE: I've often thought if God is a thought, and everybody in the Universe stopped thinking of God at the same moment, would He exist? None of this started manifesting in my conscious mind until after I had the NDE. It was just a total, total change in who I was. In the beginning I was afraid of who I was. Now I find it intriguing sometimes. People will say, "You didn't used to be like that." At first I was afraid, and now I say, "Well, tell me what I was like. I'd like to know who I was then." But yet people who didn't know me well still see me as who I was, thinking I'm still the same person. They don't see who I am. It's hard to explain. You had to be very close to see the change in the personality.

Dianne had changed so that her children asked Scott who this woman was he had brought home from the hospital. "You took one woman to the hospital and brought another one home," they said. Dianne was changed to her family, and they were different for her.

The first year of recovery, Dianne spent in the basement reading. She says she was afraid of life before her NDE. "Anyone who stays at home caring for little kids has to be afraid." It was just as hard for Dianne to be with people after the NDE, though for a different reason. In the aftermath of the NDE personal boundaries are expanded and sensitivities to noxious environments increased. A period of solitude is necessary to readjust. Dianne's retirement to the basement is the closest many can get to going to the desert. Dianne was on a personal and spiritual search, and temporarily needed time out. That was her work.

Slowly she came up and out. At first it took an act of will. She decided to do something she had wanted to do for a long time. She signed up for a Yoga class.

Then the universe, responding to the new Dianne, began to call her out. First the Yoga Center asked her to be on their Board. Then she was asked to supervise her daughter's cheerleading squad. Dianne is constantly amazed by these requests. She doesn't yet see her new self as others do, as energetic, competent and bright. Perhaps her intelligence and reawakened interest in reading will enable her to go to college and pursue a course of study that will fulfill her purpose.

Dianne has yet to discover what that is. Her present interest is in alternative healing. Dianne still has lupus, but is able to control it by mentally sending light to the affected areas.

Dianne has discovered she can also heal others, and read their hearts, minds and futures. She continues to converse with the being she met during her NDE.

Initially, Dianne said, she got calls from friends who wanted answers, and she gave them. Now she doesn't. "What if I'm wrong?" she said. "Besides, I think I have something more important to do."

Dianne has inner strength, intelligence and a caring spouse. Through her own efforts, she is in successful recovery. Others may not be so fortunate.

> DIANNE: That transition period, that year after coming home from the hospital was worse than the disease itself, psychologically. It was the worst I have ever been in my life mentally, and there was no help. There was nobody to help you. I would tell the doctor: "I feel like there is somebody living inside me and I don't know who that person is." And this person would come out and scream and yell. And immediately the response, "Well maybe we should start those Valiums now."
>
> I'd say, "No, I don't want to take Valium, please tell me what can I do?" Don't send you to a counselor, don't send you to a support group! How do you live? How do you live!

Dianne is learning to live for perhaps the first time in her life. She knew, like other NDErs, that she couldn't go to just any counselor. "They wouldn't believe me," she said. Instead, she seemed instinctively to know what she needed — a time of solitude and reflection, care in choosing her friends, work at understanding herself, her life and her purpose. It wasn't easy.

Chapter 2
Grace

Grace met me at the door in a simple slack and sweater outfit. She looks younger than her fifty-nine years despite the difficult recovery from severe head injuries incurred during the accident, nine years ago, that precipitated her NDE. A slight stiffness of gait and occasional stuttering speech are the only clues, to the casual observer, that Grace had once been "brain dead."

Like others, Grace initially had no memory of events prior to her NDE. Friends had to tell her what had happened. As she speaks, Grace seems to glow with an inner light.

GRACE: And I asked all kinds of questions about it and I found out that I was on my way to a fellowship meeting about half-past seven in the evening, and I crossed Penfield Road. A car coming down Penfield Road was going very fast. They did a study afterwards, and he had to be doing a minimum of seventy miles an hour. He struck me on the passenger side and carried me down the road about three hundred yards, up over a curb and up on a fire hydrant. The police had to cut the top off my car to get me out. And they said I had some heartbeat and breathing at the time they got me out, but by the time they got me to the hospital I had no life functions at all. The hospital report said I had no brain stem function until the morning of the third day.

After I got my memory, after the accident, after I got home, I thought about it. I decided that sometime in those two days, when I had no brain stem function, was when I must have had my NDE. Because if it had been ten years earlier, before they passed the law defining brain death, they would have buried me. But because they had to prove brain death, they had to put me on the EEG. It showed no brainwave pattern, but some intermittent electrical activity, and so they had to keep me around.

I was in a coma for three weeks, and remember none of that at all. When I came home from the hospital was when I started to remember again. I remember every single instance of my NDE, at that time. I've forgotten some of it now, but at the time I remembered every single instance. And I remembered nothing else.

When we came home, I didn't even know my own children. My husband said, "Aren't you going to say hello to your boys?" I looked at them, and they could have been slightly familiar to me, like neighborhood children.

I didn't know them. So I remembered nothing else, but I remembered every detail of my NDE.

The doctor told my husband I would be nothing but a vegetable, and to find a nursing facility where I would be kept the rest of my life. So he brought me home to be with the children for a little while 'til he could find a facility to have me put in before I disappeared for good. I had a four year old, and he felt the kids needed to see me around the house, before I took off again.

The kids started to teach me things: what table utensils were, how to use them and what they were called, and how to use a hairbrush. They taught me how to put my shoes on. In the next two weeks, they literally taught me how to get dressed. When he found out I could learn things, he said, "I'm not putting you in a nursing home." So I gradually started to learn over the next two years, over again, just like a newborn does.

Of course in those days there was no therapy. It was something like two or three years after my accident that New York recognized brain injuries. So after my accident there was no therapy. That's why they said I'd never be anything but a vegetable. I just felt the Lord didn't want me to come back to be a vegetable. I kept pushing and trying and doing, until I accomplished everything that had to be done. People used to shake their heads in disbelief. To this day, no one with the severity of head injury that I had could possibly have had the recovery that I had. And I kept telling them, "It's the Lord that did it. I put my hand in His every day, and He leads me in the right way to walk. It's Him, not me." The doctors, of course, don't believe it. They shake their heads.

These are not the words of secondhand faith. Her healing and strength derive from her continuing relationship with her Lord, whom she met in her heavenly experience. Grace described to me what happened during the two days of "death."

GRACE: It started as I was walking on a hill like one of the Finger Lakes. I was thinking to myself what a beautiful day it was. I noticed a clear spot near the top of the hill and I thought, "I wonder what's on the top of the hill?" I started to walk up to the top to see what was on the other side. I was conscious of myself. I can remember being stuck on my feet by the weeds and things I was walking through. I looked to see why my feet were being pricked, and I saw I had sandals on. And I said to myself, "You dummy, why did you wear sandals for your walk?" And I was admiring the tree, and the sky and the deep valley, things like that. It was really pretty.

When I got up to the top of the hill, there was a sort of path or lane. It wasn't paved or anything, but it was fairly wide. I looked along the track and it curved away from me, and I saw someone coming around the curve. And I thought, I wonder if this is someone I should hide from. I thought very carefully about whether this was someone I should not have see me.

In looking, I realized it was someone I loved that loved me. Just as he came around the curve, I ran up to him to take his hand, and we started walking down the path in the direction he was originally going. Then I decided to take his other hand, and I walked across in front of him and I saw his whole face, his eyes. It was his full face, his human face and the eyes. When I saw his eyes, I knew it was the Lord. And I took His hand, and we were walking along the path slowly, and I said, "Do you love me?" because that had always been a fear, that I was always doing things wrong and the Lord wouldn't love me. So I said, "Do you love me?" and He filled every single fiber of my being with a perfect love. I mean I was filled right up to the top with the most perfect love.

I remember asking how could you love me when I did. . . and I began going through all the wrongs that I did in the recent past. And right away the feeling of love I got from Him turned to total forgiveness. Afterwards, not at the time, but afterwards when I thought back on it, I remember thinking, of course, it was perfect love, and perfect love would have complete forgiveness. All I have to do is be internally very sorry for having done something, and He's forgiven me. And that's the perfect love that comes from the Lord.

Since the NDE, I still do things wrong. I'm human after all [laughs]. I still do things that I don't think are right, and that I'm sorry for afterwards; but I don't have to be upset or beat myself over the head for it. I talk to Him and let him know I feel sincerely bad about it, ask Him to help me have the strength to change that action. Then I'm totally forgiven. And I know how much He loves each and every one of us, regardless. I know it.

Guilt, that residue of conditional love, dissolves in the unconditional love of the Light, or Lord. The Love that filled her in heaven, Grace maintains, is available for every one of us, not merely reserved for Christians. Grace retains the universality of the NDE while remaining Christian. She could not, however, long remain in heaven.

GRACE: When we first started walking, all of a sudden we came to the edge of the lane or path. There was something there that stopped us that was like a stream of fog or something like that. I can remember trying very hard to see into it, to see what it was made of, and I realized I was looking for planets. Then my mind started looking for buildings on a planet, then I was looking for people. I realized that was where I came from, and I should be there. I didn't want to leave where I was, next to the Lord.

I had a very strong feeling that I had to go through or into that mist. I didn't know enough to call it a barrier. That came to me later in the NDE studies with the University of Connecticut. [Grace was interviewed by near-death researchers at U. Conn.] At the time I called it a stream, and I thought, "Oh, it's narrow, I can jump over it. That's what I'll do, I'll jump over it." And immediately it became as wide as a very big river. Then I thought,

"You know how to swim. Look for a place that's not fast-flowing or too misty and you can swim across at that point." The minute I thought that, we weren't at that barrier any more, we were over back on the path, and he was over down on the other side of the hill we had climbed.

I thought at first He was just walking through some flowers and flowering shrubs. And I began to realize there were people there. Then I thought it was children, after I looked carefully. Then I thought I should be there with Him, but a strong feeling came; no, stay where you are. He didn't bring you with Him, so stay where you are.

So I sat down on the plain, and I thought, with fear, there's something coming down that road that I wouldn't want to encounter. Then I thought, "Why should you be afraid? You can see Him. So long as you're near Him, there is absolutely nothing to fear, and you can be content as can be." So I sat there. As long as He was close, I was prepared to just sit there. As soon as I knew I was content to just sit there and be near Him, we were back at the barrier again.

Then there was another episode when we went away from the barrier. He started to talk to me, and He was discussing with me things that I had done in the past, how I reacted to it, giving me strong feelings about how He wished I had reacted to it, or how good it was I had reacted in that way. We went through quite a lot of interplay there, feelings.

And then there was one time when I was very upset with my husband and ready to leave him, and when that came into my mind, we were all of a sudden back at the barrier again. I looked at that stream of fog, and I turned to Him to say, "Lord, why are we here again?" When I did, I thought I saw an expression on His face of disappointment. I mean I don't know that it was there, but my feeling was that He had a look of disappointment. And I put my head on His chest and said, "Oh, Lord, I never want to disappoint you. I only want to please you." And that was the end of my experience.

Grace goes to the barrier between life and death several times. Atypically, she is on the wrong side of the stream and must recross to enter life. Her crossing is successful only after two critical episodes; she submits to her Lord's will and remembers some unfinished business in her marital relationship.

Grace and I sat in the clutter of packing boxes as we spoke. Typical of many NDErs, Grace's husband had asked for a separation. She was about to depart from their lovely split-level colonial for a condominium. Apparently the reason for the separation was not the need to care for Grace during her recovery, but her newly discovered assertiveness and her changed priorities. He was simply no longer her god.

GRACE: I have not been assertive with my husband through our married life. When I had my NDE, we had been married somewhere between twenty and twenty-five years. I had gotten into the habit over the years of doing everything he told me to do. And if I didn't do what he wanted, or thought differently, I would either have a fight with him, which would be a bad thing; or I would be a naughty girl, not doing what I was told. I think I unconsciously acted as if my husband was my god.

I withdrew from church for ten or fifteen years, until I had two children. After five miscarriages and many years of not being able to get pregnant, I had two children. I had one at forty and one at age forty-five, and I was so grateful to him. I was sure He had given me a couple of miracles, which of course children always are. I was positive about it, and I did go back to church fairly often, after my last one was born. Now I can't imagine going through a day without being with the Lord.

"Let me say what you want me to say, do what you want me to do. Your will only." I start my day that way. People say how can you go on doing all the things you're doing and be so strong, when right before Christmas your husband asked you for a separation? I don't believe it's a matter of strength. I follow the serenity prayer. I use it. I change what I can, and that's only me [laughs]. Where the wisdom comes in is to know the difference, and that's really what I'm doing. I accept whenever I can't make a change, and make one where I can. And it's working out beautifully. My lawyer even thinks my husband and I will be back together again.

My husband has been saying these last five months, that before the accident I would do what he wanted. I took over everything. I did the whole budget. I did it all. He got whatever he wanted, and I made it work within the budget. So he was used to my handling everything his way. After the accident, I began doing things for me because I felt I was following the Lord's will. I was unable to do some of the things I did before, because mentally I haven't got it. He had to take over a lot of it. But I didn't read his mind any more. I didn't say, "He wants it like this, so I'll do it like this. I'll fix it so he gets his way. I was busy doing it the Lord's way, and that meant doing for me too; taking time to enjoy life, taking out a half-hour to enjoy the birds or whatever. I could do it my way because I felt that's the way I should do it at that time. It wasn't what my husband wanted. I stopped saying, "Oh, what will David say? What will David say?" I stopped putting him first and started putting the Lord first and me second, then my husabnd, and then the kids.

Grace is not the only NDEr whose husband has resented losing his divine status. She has, however, discovered wisdom as well as compassion.

GRACE: You see they're too human. They think they're in charge. So many humans have the biggest problem in life, I'm beginning to realize, because they think of themselves as little gods, even unconsciously. And they think it has to be their way, and they're going to take over and control. God is the only one who is in control, and we have to do things His way. If I'm walking the wrong path, things go wrong. If I'm walking the right path, everything works beautifully.

> For the last month, it has been frustrating because things are slow, but everything has been working out perfectly. I have absolutely no fear now; and I know it's because it was replaced with faith. No fear of anything. Of course, I'm not foolish either. I'm not going to walk down a very bad neighborhood street at midnight and ask for something to happen. I have to use my common sense. He's leading me in the right direction, and nothing that isn't His will is going to happen.

Through her trust in her Lord, rediscovered assertiveness, rearranged priorities, and just plain hard work, things are working out well for Grace. In the three years since I've known her, her healing has been dramatic. Her speech is more clear. She drives at night without getting lost. She handled the details of the condo choice and purchase alone, as well as most of the packing and much of the moving. While incapable of holding a job, Grace manages an independent life. Care of her ailing mother, helping others with head injuries and communicating her experience whenever she can, fills what spare time she has after taking care of herself. Soon after her recent move, Grace took a long-awaited three week train ride across Canada. She is overjoyed to be able to do the things she has always wanted to do, and believes her husband gave her a gift of freedom.

Grace wasn't always submissive. Like Dianne, an early sense of self and assertion was lost somewhere in childhood, and rediscovered during the NDE. Though most of Grace's pre-NDE memory is lost, she was able to recount two traumatic incidents from childhood: a presumed drowning and a sexual assault. These, like Dianne's, aren't arbitrary memories. During her NDE, two incidents relate to these other memories — when she attempts to swim the barrier, and when she encounters a fearful presence on the path.

Grace grew up on Irondequoit Bay, an inlet of Lake Ontario. One day the family was taking an uneventful boatride until Grace decided to swim for shore. As her parents were examining an ailing motor, Grace saw a group of friends on the shore and jumped in, not knowing, she said, that you needed to know how to swim. Her parents panicked and called the police, who began dragging the bay for Grace's body. Grace was safely on the beach with her friends, having managed to dog-paddle to shore. Afterward, her mother gave her swimming lessons, which she turned into a profession in later life. Throughout her married life Grace taught swimming at a Rochester, New York YMCA, and scuba diving in Syracuse, where her husband was employed by General Electric.

Another incident was traumatic for Grace as well as her family, but during this she also discovered instincts and strengths which enabled her to survive. One day, as Grace was walking to school, a man asked her to come down the railroad tracks to show her something. He drew her behind one of the buildings and began to "become familiar with me."

Repeated cries of "no" availed little, so Grace kicked him in his "privates." When she got to school, she asked the nuns if she could go into Church. There she talked to Jesus about it and asked Him if she should tell her mother. On returning home from school, she told her mother, who called the police. Questions followed, and according to Grace, that was the end of the incident.

Grace says the incident bothered her only momentarily. However, recent findings in childhood sexual abuse suggest that even a tiny bit can damage a child. It is possible that, for Grace, the feeling of being loved and good was lost in that event, and recovered dramatically during her NDE. She has since lost all fear and discovered a new sense of self — one that is loved and accepted for its own sake, not for its accomplishments or beautiful body. Grace now sees her soul in the mirror, and likes what she sees.

> GRACE: That's why my husband wants a separation. I am not the same woman he married. I look in the mirror, and I know that's not the person that I remember. The person I remember looked different from the one I see in the mirror. So when I look in the mirror, I'm looking at my skin to see if I need to do something. I don't look at my image because it's not me. I thought I was a physically prettier person than I see in the mirror now. On top of that I see an expression that surprises me all the time, that I didn't seem to have before. It seemed the physical appearance used to be important, and I had to look like I was a very pretty special person. It showed on my face. Now what I see is a benign, calm, grateful expression, and I know that it is the new me. I don't have to be that special looking person. Inside is much more important.

Like the mystics, Grace has rediscovered the soul and realized its value. Grace didn't see the Light during her NDE, but the soul light gleaming in her eyes gives her a new beauty.

Grace is "mystical" in other ways as well. She, like John of the Cross, has relinquished personal memory, intellect and will. During her NDE she stopped thinking. Now the clarity, simplicity and wisdom of her speech suggests to me the divine intelligence that daily provides Grace with inspiration, information, guidance, and strength.

> GRACE: As far as hearing His voice, I don't really hear His voice. I tried to remember after the accident, whether He spoke to me the way I spoke to Him, and I cannot remember His lips moving. I know that I spoke to Him a few times, but He read my thoughts. As quick as I could think things, whamo! So most of the time I was not speaking to Him. I was just thinking things, and He knew it. I don't remember His lips moving, so I don't think He spoke to me. I just knew what He put in my head. And so now, I don't get a voice still. When I'm meditating He does sometimes get through to me very plainly. What I get is a really, really strong mental picture, and

an urge to go in a particular direction. And then I say, "Lord, is that the way you want me to go?" and the urge will get for a minute real, real strong. And I know that's the answer.

It's hard to put into words. As I say, human language does not express the spiritual. I feel continually grateful that I and some other NDErs have this gift. And I continually say, "Why me, Lord?" And then I realize that every single one of us is offered the same gift. Only those who accept it does it come to.

Through inspiration, Grace has received an understanding of the world to come similar to Howard's and other near-death prophetic visions.

GRACE: I have no doubt that Christ is going to come back to His world in His time. And those of us who are chosen to be with Him, will be with Him on this earth when His Kingdom comes.

At first I knew just my NDE, because I didn't have a well-functioning brain the first couple of years. After the brain started to connect synapses and started to work well again, I began to have that very strong belief. I just knew that the three persons in one was an actuality and that the Lord was going to come into His kingdom and live with us here on earth.

I asked Grace about the difference between this world and the Kingdom.

GRACE: There is a very big difference in emotions, and your being in one place and all of a sudden you're in another place, and this sort of thing. But so far as the physical, the hills, the trees, the valleys, it was so much like my NDE. I had the sense that while I was walking with him up the path we were on earth, but it was a different world. Yes, maybe it was something like the earth, but it wasn't the earth as we know it. My feelings were very intense and very real and clear to me.

As I said, the trees were in leaf and bloom, and flowers were in bloom, and the grass was soft and green and beautiful. I did feel the weedy section, but of course it would be a natural world. But because it is the Lord's Kingdom man will have a different place on it than he has now. We will do whatever the Lord wants us to do in enjoying the world, sharing with each other, and continual interplay between people. I can't help but believe that the love He has for us is going to be with those of us who will be chosen to share with Him His Kingdom. And we'll love everyone the same way, so we'll share everything with each other the same way. And the world and all its riches will be there for us to take part of in any way we want to.

We won't have the restrictions of humanity. We'll be free spirits with all of the physical attributes that we could possibly enjoy in a physical world. We won't be physical bodies, so we won't need to eat. We will, in the final days, be in bodies, you know. Like its been written in the Bible, we will get our bodies back when we rise from the dead, when the Lord takes over the Kingdom. We will be able to eat and drink, but we won't have to. It won't be a physical requirement. We will be spirits in a physical form, enjoying everything just like Adam and Eve were meant to. And to me that's what I mean by three-dimensional. We see now in three dimensions, while others still see only in two. When I tell them, they look at me like I don't have a healed brain.

Apocalyptic tales of the coming of the Kingdom such as Grace's are easy to dismiss. They have been circulating for thousands of years, and we appear to inhabit the same old world. Howard and Grace are not alone, however, in predicting imminent catastrophe and the eventual establishment of a more spiritual state on earth. Perhaps it will at last be a reality. Who knows.

The imagery of Grace's NDE was Christian, and she returned to a welcoming Christian church. Though her interpretation of the event is, therefore, Christian, the ideas have a universal application. Grace insists her gifts are available to everyone, and she spends her spare time sharing her message of hope, her miraculous recovery, and her spiritual light.

Grace is simple, but with a sophistication beyond the simplicity of the mentally impaired. The impression Grace leaves with those who know her is of purity as well as simplicity. She leads a simple, divinely guided, even joyful life in the midst of personal tragedy. Her recovery hasn't been easy. She has had to struggle to return from a vegetative state, as well as convince an incredulous world of her sanity. Grace has spent time in a psychiatric setting diagnosed as a manic-depressive. As Grace says, when she is with her Lord she feels wonderful. When she returns to earth and realizes the magnitude of her problems, she despairs. Do we blame her? However, in the course of her therapy Grace eventually encountered a sympathetic psychiatrist. He not only accepted and affirmed her experience, but has given Grace additional courage to become her new assertive, independent, deeply spiritual self.

Chapter 3
Howard

I first met Howard Storm two years ago at a Near-Death Conference. He told the conferees about his NDE and I listened intently, drawn to Howard because of the divine love that shines in his eyes, and the balance he has achieved in the five years since his experience. When we finally met, I asked if he would tell his story and share his successful coping skills with the readers of *Mysticism and Madness*. He agreed, and will tell you in his own written words about his NDE.

Howard comes from a privileged background. He grew up in an affluent suburb of Boston and attended college in California. It was the 60s and he tried drugs. Now he says, he doesn't even drink. It would spoil his divine "high."

Howard's affluent upbringing came at a price. He rarely saw the father who worked two jobs to provide "extras" for the family. Howard took his anger at this "abandonment" out on the track. He was a star athlete. During his NDE, however, the light beings he encountered were uninterested in his medals. The only important event of his teen years, from their perspective, was the night he comforted his sister after she had been physically abused.

After college, Howard became an art professor. He had achieved tenure by the early age of thirty-two. Howard appeared to have it all — a great personality, and achievement by the standards of the world. Since his NDE, however, Howard says he only has contempt for the person he was before. Like many other NDErs Howard was healed of old hurts and changed dramatically in an experience that happened in Paris. Unlike most NDErs, however, Howard's heavenly adventure was preceded by a trip to hell.

Howard was in Paris leading an art tour when, one day, he collapsed in his hotel room. "Suddenly," he said, "I felt as though I'd been shot. There was a searing pain in the middle of my stomach. My knees collapsed and I sank to the floor. I held my gut and screamed with pain."

A doctor was called who examined Howard and declared he had a perforated duodenum. Howard was given morphine and taken to the hospital. After an emergency room exam he was told he needed surgery immediately or he would die. They wheeled him to a hospital room, where he remained, unattended, for hours.

HOWARD: Minute by minute the time passed. By eight-thirty that evening the pain had become completely unbearable. I'd been in that room since noon. The pain didn't come and go, but remained constant and got steadily worse. The hydrochloric acid from my stomach was leaking into my abdominal cavity and literally eating me up from the inside. I kept thinking, this is not how it's supposed to end. I was fading away in a Paris hospital and they were indifferent to my agony. What would happen to my wife, my two children, my paintings, my house, my gardens? I had grown so weak I could barely lift my head or speak. [My wife]. . .looked exhausted. I didn't want to tell her that I knew the end was near. It began to get very dark outside.

Sometime around nine o'clock one of the nurses came into the room. They said the doctor had gone home and the operation couldn't be performed until the next morning. I knew I couldn't survive until then. I was later told by American doctors that after the initial episode my life expectancy was about five hours. Ten hours had now passed. I had fought as long and as hard as I could to stay alive. I had nothing left to give.

I knew that I was dying, and that dying was the only way out of the pain. To die seemed like the easiest thing in the world. All I would have to do was stop fighting. . . Saying something to myself like, let it end now, I closed my eyes. I knew that what would happen next would be the end of any kind of thoughts or existence. I knew that to be absolutely true. The idea of any kind of life after death never crossed my mind. I then drifted into darkness, like falling asleep, and it felt wonderful.

I don't know how much time elapsed after I had gone completely unconscious. The next thing I knew was that I felt like I was standing up. I opened my eyes to see why I was having this sensation. I was standing between the two hospital beds in the room. This wasn't what I expected, this wasn't right. Why was I still alive? I wanted oblivion. Then I looked at my roommate . . .and his eyes were closed. I turned and looked at Beverly [my wife] sitting in the chair next to my bed. She was motionless, staring at the floor. I spoke to her, but she didn't seem to hear. Then I noticed that I [my body] was lying on the bed. I looked down at my hands, arms, torso, legs and feet. It was my body, but it looked so meaningless, like a husk. I stood there looking at it. Everything I thought was me was standing there. I was all there, intact. Everything that I could see from the neck down was right there. Yet I was looking at a thing that was my body, and it just didn't have that much meaning to me.

I wanted this to be a dream, and I kept saying to myself, "This has got to be a dream." But I knew that it wasn't a dream. I became aware that strangely I felt more alert, more aware, more alive than I had ever felt in my entire life. All my senses were extremely acute. Everything felt tingly and alive. The floor was cool and my bare feet felt moist and clammy. This had to be real. I squeezed my fists and was amazed how much I was feeling in my hands just by making a fist. I felt my body with my hands in several places and everything was as it should be. I still had pain in my stomach but not nearly as severe as before.

It struck me then that I had gone crazy. Somehow I had split my personality. Somehow I was schizophrenic, completely mad. And all I wanted was just to get out of life. I wanted desperately to contact Beverly, and I started yelling for her to say something, but she remained frozen. I turned to my roommate and he, too, seemed to be totally ignoring me. I yelled, "Why are you just ignoring me?" Nothing worked. I became increasingly upset as anger, fear, and confusion filled me.

Off in the distance outside the room, in the hall, I heard voices calling me by name. They were pleasant voices, male and female, young and old, calling me in English. None of the hospital staff spoke English this well and they couldn't pronounce the name "Howard." I was confused. Beverly didn't appear to hear them. I asked who they were and what they wanted. They said, "Come on out here." "Let's go." "Hurry up." "I can't," I said. "I'm sick. Something's the matter with me; something's wrong in here." They said, "We can get you fixed up if you hurry. Don't you want to get better? Don't you want help?"

I was in a strange hospital in a strange country, in a very bizarre situation, and I was leery of those voices. They seemed irritated by my attempts to find out who they were. The hall looked strange as I moved closer to the door. I had a feeling that if I lost the room, which was vivid and real and contained my wife, my roommate, and my body, it might be impossible to get back. But I couldn't communicate with my wife and I couldn't communicate with my roommate. The voices said, "We can't help you if you don't come out here." After more futile questions, I decided my best bet was to follow them rather than remain in torment in a room where everyone ignored me.

I stepped, with a good deal of anxiety, out into the hall. The area seemed to be bright but very hazy like a TV screen with terrible reception. I couldn't make out any details. It was much like being in a plane passing through thick clouds. The people were off in the distance, and I couldn't see them clearly. But I could tell that they were male and female, tall and short, old and young, but no children. As I tried to get close to them to identify them, they quickly withdrew deeper into the fog. So I had to follow into the fog deeper and deeper. I could never get closer than ten or fifteen feet from them. I had lots of questions. Who were they? What did they want? Where did they want me to go? Why wasn't I back there in my body? What was the matter with my wife? How could this be real? They wouldn't answer anything. The only response was insisting that I hurry up and follow them. They told me repeatedly that my pain was meaningless and unnecessary. "Pain is bullshit," they said. So I started following them, in great emotional distress, shuffling along in my bare feet, with the pain in my belly, feeling very much alive.

I knew that I had a problem with my abdominal area, and it hurt a little. Before I had left my body and was still conscious, it was difficult to move anything. To move my tongue caused pain. Every breath I took hurt because it moved my diaphragm, which agitated my abdominal cavity. As I walked along, there wasn't nearly the pain that there was before.

Every time I hesitated, they cajoled me to follow faster. They repeated the promise that if I followed them my pain would end. We walked on and on. My repeated inquiries were rebuffed with anxious insistence about the need for haste.

During the journey I attempted to count how many there were and to figure out something about their individual identities, but I couldn't. The fog thickened as we went on and it became darker. They moved around me and their numbers seemed to be increasing. I became confused about the direction we were taking. I knew that we had been travelling for miles, but I occasionally had the strange ability to look back and see the hospital room. My body was still there lying motionless on the bed. . . . My perspective at these times was as if I were floating above the room looking down. It seemed millions and millions of miles away.

All the while we were walking, I was trying to pick up some clues as to where we were going by what we were walking on. The floor or ground had no features. There was no incline or decline nor any variation in texture. It was like walking on a smooth, slightly damp, cool floor. I found that very disturbing. How could this same unvarying plane go on forever? When would we go uphill or downhill? The only awareness I sometimes had was a sense that we might be descending.

I also couldn't make out how much time was passing. There was a profound sense of timelessness. This was strange because as a teacher I had always been able to estimate when I had talked for a certain length of time. I did know that it seemed as if we had been walking a long while. I kept asking when we were going to get there. "I'm sick," I said. "I can't do this." They beame increasingly angry and sarcastic. "If you'd quit moaning and groaning, we'd get there," they said. "Move it. Let's go. Hurry up." The more questioning and suspicious I was, the more antagonistic and rude and authoritarian they became. They began to make jokes about my bare rear end which wasn't covered by my hospital dicky and about how pathetic I was. I knew they were talking about me, but when I tried to find out exactly what they were saying they would say, "Shh, he can hear you, he can hear you."

All my communication with them took place verbally just as ordinary human communication occurs. They didn't appear to know what I was thinking, and I didn't know what they were thinking. What was increasingly obvious was that they were liars and help was farther away the more I stayed with them.

Before the journey began, the physical pain was intense, but now my emotional experience had become unendurable. Hours ago, I had hoped to die and end the torment of life. Now things were worse as I was forced by a mob of unfriendly and cruel people toward some unknown destination in the darkness. They began shouting and hurling insults at me, demanding that I hurry along. And they refused to answer any question. The more miserable I became, the more enjoyment they derived from my distress.

An enormous sense of dread was building within me. This experience was sickeningly real. In some subtle ways, I was more aware and sensitive than I had ever been before in my entire life. Everything that was happening was not possible, yet it was happening. This was not a dream or hallucination, but I wished it were. I was feeling very frightened, exhausted, cold, lost, and in physical agony. It was clear that the help they had first promised was just a ruse to trick me into following. I was reluctant to go further, but any hesitation brought abuse and insults. They told me we were almost there, to shut up and take a few more steps. A few of the voices attempted a conciliatory tone which amused the others. Among themselves the mood was very excited and triumphant.

For a long time I had been walking with my gaze on my feet. When I looked up I was horrified to discover that we were in complete darkness. The absolute hopelessness of my situation overwhelmed me. I told them I would go no further, to leave me alone, and that they were liars. I could feel their breath on me as they shouted and snarled ridicules and insults. Then they began to pull and shove me about. With that I began to fight back. A wild orgy of frenzied taunting, screaming and hitting ensued. I fought like a wild man. As I swung and kicked at them, they bit and tore at me. All the while it was obvious that they were having great fun. Even though I couldn't see anything in the darkness, I was aware there were what seemed like hundreds of them all around and over me. My attempts to fight back only provoked greater merriment. They began to physically humiliate me in the most degrading ways. As I continued to fight on and on, I was aware that they weren't in any hurry to win. They were playing with me just as a cat plays with a mouse. Every new assault brought howls of cacophony. Then at some point, they began to tear off pieces of my flesh. To my horror I realized I was being taken apart and eaten alive, slowly, so that their entertainment would last as long as possible.

I want to reiterate that what was happening was extremely real. In that darkness, I knew that my senses were heightened. While I couldn't see in the now total blackness, every sound and every physical sensation registered with horrifying intensity.

At no time did I ever have any sense that the beings who seduced and attacked me were anything other than human beings. The best way I can describe them is to think of the worst imaginable person stripped of every impulse to do good. Some of them seemed to be able to tell others what to do, but I had no sense of any structure or hierarchy in an organizational sense. They didn't appear to be controlled or directed by anyone. Basically they were a mob of beings totally driven by unbridled cruelty and passions.

In the darkness I had extensive physical contact with them. When they swarmed over me, their bodies felt exactly as human bodies do except for two characteristics. They had very sharp, hard fingernails. My impression was also that their teeth were longer than normal, but it's hard to say. I've never been bitten by a normal human being before. During our struggle I noticed that they seemed to feel no pain. Other than that they appeared

to possess no special nonhuman or superhuman abilities. Although during my initial experience with them I assumed that they were clothed, in our intimate physical contact I never felt any clothing whatsoever.

Eventually I became too badly torn up and too weak to continue to resist. Most of the beings gave up in disappointment because I was no longer amusing, but a few still picked and gnawed at me and ridiculed me for no longer being any fun. By this time I had been pretty much taken apart. In that state I lay there in the darkness.

I am aware in looking back that there was much more involved in this part of the experience that I haven't described. At the time I was caught up in the emotionally harrowing experience of fighting for my life. That's what I recall most intensely. There are many details that I simply don't remember. In fact, much that occurred was simply too gruesome and disturbing to recall. I've spent the last three years consciously trying to suppress much of it. Right after the experience, whenever I did remember those details I became highly disturbed and would require hours to calm down.

At some point, I was aware of the strange sensation of hearing a voice which seemed like it came from my chest. It was my voice, but it clearly wasn't a thought from my mind. The voice that was my voice but that wasn't part of my conscious mind said, "Pray." And I remember distinctly that my conscious mind said, Why? What a stupid idea. That doesn't work. That's a cop out. This is a guy lying on the ground in the darkness surrounded by what appeared to be dozens if not hundreds and hundreds of vicious creatures who had just torn him up. The situation seemed utterly hopeless, and I seemed beyond any possible help whether I believed in God or not.

The voice said again emphatically, "Pray to God." I wasn't sure how to do that. Praying, for me, had always been something I watched adults doing. It was something fancy and had to be done just so. I tried to remember prayers from my childhood experiences in Sunday School. Gingerly, I murmured bits of the Twenty-Third Psalm and the Lord's Prayer and the Pledge of Allegiance and *God Bless America* and whatever churchly sounding phrases that came to mind. To my incredible surprise the beings which were around me were horrified and incited by what I was doing. It was as if I was throwing boiling oil on them. They screamed at me, "There is no God. Who do you think you're talking to? Nobody can hear you." But at the same time they started backing away. I could hear their voices in the darkness, and they were getting more and more distant. I realized that mumbling things about God was actually driving them away. I became a little more forceful with what I was saying. As they were retreating, they became more rabid, cursing and screaming that what I was saying was worthless and that I was a coward. But in a short amount of time they all retreated back into the gloom.

Then I was completely alone, physically dismembered yet painfully alive and real, in this dark and horrible place. I had no idea where I was. As I was walking with these people, I thought we were in some foggy part of the Paris hospital. In time I realized we had left Paris and gone somewhere else. Now I didn't know if I was even in the world. But I did know that I was here, I was real, all my senses worked too painfully well. I didn't know how I had arrived here. There was no direction to follow even if I had been physically able to move. The agony that I had suffered during the day was nothing compared to what I was feeling now. I even hoped that one or two of the beings would come back, that I could be with them. The loneliness and complete despair was the lowest deep depression. I knew then that this was the absolute end of my existence, and it was more horrible than anything I could possibly have imagined. It would have been much better to have died in the hospital than in this despicable place. I felt like a match whose flame had spent and the ember was slowly dying away to nothing. That's how little strength I had left.

Then in my consciousness for the first time in my adult life a song started going through my head, "Jesus loves me————." I didn't remember the rest of the verse, only the tune and those few words. We had sung that nursery school rhyme in the Sunday School that I attended as a child. What that meant to me was that somewhere out there in that darkness there is something that is good and something that wanted me. I didn't have any theological concept about what that meant. It was a recollection from my Sunday School days growing up in a Protestant church. God/Jesus, one and the same, loves me. I wanted someone to love me. I thought about how prayers to God had driven the monstrous beings away. A new awareness began to dawn in me, an overwhelming belief that there really was something outside myself. For the first time in my life I knew that it was true that Jesus/God did love me. I didn't know how to express what I wanted and needed, so with my last bit of strength I yelled out into the darkness, "Jesus, save me." I yelled that with every bit of energy that I had left.

Off in the darkness I saw a pinpoint of light like the faintest star in the sky. I wondered why I hadn't seen it before. The star was getting brighter and brighter. At first I thought it might be some phenomenon like a meteor. Then it dawned on me that it was moving toward me at what apparently was an enormous rate of speed. As it closed in I realized that I was right in its path and I might be run over. But I couldn't take my eyes off it, because emanating from the light was more intensity and more beauty than I had ever seen before in my life. Almost immediately the light was very close. I realized then that while it was indescribably brilliant, it wasn't light at all. It was a living entity, a luminous being approximately eight feet in diameter and oval in shape. Its brilliance and intensity penetrated my body. In a very vivid and beautiful experience I slowly rose up with no effort into the light, and the pieces of my body somehow assembled. Looking at myself, I could see that all my wounds had disappeared, and I had become whole and well.

The luminous entity that embraced me knew me intimately and began to communicate a tremendous sense of knowledge. I knew that he knew everything about me and I was being unconditionally loved and accepted. It then totally enveloped me, and I realized that he had a certain substance,

more dense than water, but not solid. He was a concentrated field of energy, radiant in splendor indescribable, except to say goodness and love. This was more loving than one can imagine.

But it was loving me with overwhelming power. After what I had been through to be completely known, accepted, and intensely loved by this being of light surpassed anything I had known or could have imagined. I began to cry and the tears kept coming and coming.

I rose upward, enveloped in that luminous being. Gradually at first, and then like a rocket travelling at great speed, we shot out of that dark and detestable place. I sensed that we traversed an enormous distance although very little time seemed to elapse. Then, off in the distance, I saw a vast area of illumination that looked like a galaxy. In the center there was an enormously bright concentration. Outside the center countless millions of spheres of light were flying about entering and leaving what was a great Beingness at the center.

The radiance emanating from the luminous spheres contained exquisite colors of a range and intensity which far exceeded anything I as an artist had ever experienced. It was similar to looking at the opalescence one experiences looking into a white pearl or the brilliance in a diamond.

As we approached the great luminous center I was permeated with palpable radiation which I experienced as intense feelings and thoughts. People who had had near-death experiences, I have since learned, have described encounters with the light as being exposed to complete knowledge. Yet when they are asked what they remember, they recall few if any specifics. That's the way it was for me. At the time I felt that I was in touch with everything, but subsequently I couldn't recall the knowledge. And there was a period of time, during my presence in the great light, when I was beyond any thoughts. It is not possible to articulate the exchange that occured. Simply stated, I knew God loved me.

Eventually I began to be aware of my separate self, and I became very ashamed and afraid. How many times in my life had I denied and scoffed at the reality before me, and how many thousands of times had I used it as a curse. What incredible intellectual arrogance to use the name as an insult. I was afraid to go closer. I was also aware that the incredible intensity of the emanations might disintegrate what I still experienced as my intact physical body. The being who was supporting me, my friend, was aware of my fear and reluctance and shame. For the first time he spoke to my mind in a male voice and told me that if I was uncomfortable we didn't have to go closer. So we stopped where we were, still countless miles away from the great being.

Facing all the splendor made me acutely aware of my lowly condition. I said, "I think there's been a mistake. I don't belong here. I'm not good enough." My friend said, "We don't make mistakes. You do belong here." Then he called out in a musical tone to the luminous entities who surrounded the great center. Several came and circled around us. During what follows some came and went but normally there were five or six and sometimes as many as eight with us.

In attempting to describe this and other aspects of what happened I'm acutely aware that the words we have are simply not adequate. In describing the beings I've used the word "luminous" often rather than "light" because the emanations from those beings didn't resemble light as we experience it. When you look into a bright light the intensity hurts your eyes. The luminous beings were far brighter than a powerful spotlight, yet I could look at them as long as I wanted with no sense of discomfort. In fact the light they emanated penetrated me. I could feel it inside me and through me, and it made me feel wonderful.

To my surprise and also distress they seemed to be capable of knowing everything I was thinking. I didn't know whether I would be capable of controlling my thoughts and keeping anything secret.

We began to engage in thought exchange, conversation very natural, very easy and casual. I heard their voices clearly and individually. They each had a distinct personality with a voice, but they spoke directly to my mind, not through my ears. And they used normal, colloquial English. Everything I thought, they knew.

The Beings said, "You're upset. What can we do to help you?" "I don't belong here," I replied. "You do belong here. This is right. It's all been for this. We can appear to you in human form or in any form you want so you will be comfortable with us."

I had the sense that for them to become human meant they would have to turn down their radiance. This seemed like an insult to their glorious appearance. "NO," I said. "Please don't change into anything for me. You're more beautiful than anything I've ever seen."

They all seemed to know and understand me very well and to be completely familiar with my thoughts and my past. I didn't feel any desire to ask for someone I had known because they all knew me. Nobody could know me any better. It also didn't occur to me to try to identify them as Uncle or Grandfather. It was like going to a large gathering of relatives at Christmas and not being quite able to remember their names or who they are married to or how they are connected to you. But you do know that you are with your family. I don't know if they were related to me or not. It felt like they were closer to me than anyone I had ever known. They asked me if there was anything I wanted to know. I began asking questions and continued until I had inquired about everything I could think of.

Throughout my conversation with the luminous beings, which lasted for what seemed like a very long time, I was being physically supported by the being in whom I had been engulfed. We were in a sense completely stationary yet hanging in space. Everywhere around us were countless radiant beings, like stars in the sky, coming and going. It was like a super magnified view of a galaxy super packed with stars. And in the giant radiance of the center they were packed so densely together that individuals could not be identified. Their selves were in such harmony with the creator that they were really just one.

One of the reasons, I was told, that all the countless beings had to go back to their source was to become invigorated with this sense of harmony and oneness. Being apart for too long a time diminished them and made them feel separate. Their greatest pleasure was to go back to the sources of all life.

Our initial conversation involved them simply trying to comfort me. Something that disturbed me was that I was naked. Somewhere in the darkness I'd lost my hospital gown. I was a human being. I had a body. They told me this was okay. They were quite familiar with my anatomy. Gradually I relaxed and stopped trying to cover my privates with my hands. As we conversed they built a relationship of familiarity making it very clear that wherever I was coming from they were willing to meet me more than half way. They were willing to be completely with me as I was. Part of that was base and vulgar, which was part of my character, and some of it was spiritual.

One of my most pressing concerns was the reality of the whole experience. Real as this seemed, how could I be sure. "Search inside your mind and your feelings," they said, "and decide whether this is real or not." Methodically and carefully I examined each one of my senses. Not only were they fully operating, but they were in fact extremely enhanced. I compared what I was experiencing now to dreams and to hallucinations I had while experimenting with drugs in the sixties. What was happening now was completely unlike anything I had known before. After an intense examination of my experience, I concluded that what was happening was the most real experience of my life. I was not in some kind of fantasy, but in a superior reality beyond what can be experienced by everyday human consciousness. I knew that language didn't exist to describe it.

The beings were pleased with my recognition of the truth. They told me that in time I would be able to use the new senses I was becoming aware of and that eventually I could be as they are. Then they answered every question I ever had. Very often I didn't comprehend, and they patiently and lovingly explained things over and over with simple examples. When even this didn't work, they showed me things so that I could have a direct experience of what they were trying to communicate. This included being presented with very real images of things distant in both time and space. This went on for a very long time in my subjective experience of duration.

Howard was told by the light beings about the new world to come. According to them, God wished to usher in the Kingdom within the next two hundred years. In order to do so, God had rescinded some of the free will given to creatures, in favor of more divine control over human events. The new world order, according to Howard, will resemble some near-death descriptions of heaven. People will live in such peace and harmony and love that communication will be telepathic, travel instantaneous and the need for clothing and shelter eliminated. The lion will indeed lie down with the lamb. Harmony will exist with the created order and people will control the weather and grow plants through loving communication. While all of this may appear fantastic, they may prove to be symbols of a new order of things that differs radically from the world in which we now live. Howard says, "I don't care whether I am right. I give people hope."

HOWARD: After a long period of education I was anxious to become like one of my teachers and to be with them forever. I said, "I'm ready, I'm ready to be like you and be here forever. This is great. I love it. I love you. You're wonderful." I knew that they loved me and knew everything about me. I knew that everything was going to be okay from now on. I asked if I could get rid of my body, which was definitely a hindrance, and become a being like them with the powers they had shown me. To my great disappointment they said to me, "You're going to go back." They explained to me that I was very underdeveloped and that it would be of great benefit to return to my physical existence to learn. In my human life I would have an opportunity to grow so that the next time I was with them I would be more compatible. I would need to develop important characteristics to become like them and to be involved with the work that they do.

Some of my self-centeredness welled up and I said, "No way. I'm not going back." They said, "There are people who care about you; your wife, your children, your mother and father. You should go back for them. Your children need your help." I said, "You can help them. If you make me go back there are things that just won't work. If I go back there and make mistakes I won't be able to stand it because you've shown me I could be more loving and more compassionate and I'll forget. I'll be mean to someone or I'll do something awful to someone. I just know it's going to happen because I'm a human being. I'm going to blow it and I won't be able to stand it. I'll feel so bad I'll want to kill myself and I can't do that because life is precious. I might just go catatonic. So you can't send me back." They assured me that mistakes are an acceptable part of being human. "Go," they said, "and make all the mistakes you want. Mistakes are how you learn." As long as I tried to do what I knew was right, they said, I would be on the right path. If I made a mistake, I should fully recognize it as a mistake, then put it behind me and simply try not to make the same mistake again. The important things is to try one's best, keep one's standards of goodness and truth, and not compromise those to win people's approval. "But," I said, "mistakes make me feel bad." They said, "We love you the way you are, mistakes and all. And you can feel our forgiveness. You can feel our love any time you want to." I said, "I don't understand. How do I do that?" "Just turn inward," they said. "Just ask for our love and we'll give it to you if you ask from the heart."

I didn't give in easily. I argued that "back there" was full of problems and that here was everything I could possibly want. I questioned my ability to accomplish anything they would consider important in my world. They said the world is a beautiful expression of the Supreme Being. One can find beauty or ugliness depending on what one directs one's mind toward. They explained that the subtle and complex development of our world was beyond my comprehension, but I would be a suitable instrument for the Creator. Every part of the creation, they explained, is infinitely interesting because it is a manifestation of the Creator. A very important opportunity for me would be to explore this world with wonder and enjoyment. They never gave me a direct mission or purpose. Could I build a shrine or cathedral for God? They said those monuments were for mankind. They wanted me to live my life to love people not things. I told them I wasn't good enough to represent what I had just experienced with them on a worldly level. They assured me I would be given appropriate help whenever I might need it. All I had to do is ask.

At this point my arguments were almost exhausted. I began to think about what I might encounter immediately back in my earthly existence. I remembered the condition of my body and wondered about my medical problems. They told me my illness would be a valuable learning experience. I would eventually recover from my difficulties, but the trials and suffering involved would be important.

The luminous beings, my teachers, were very convincing. I was also acutely aware that not far away was the great Being, what I knew to be the Creator. They never said, "He wants it this way," but that was implied behind everything they said. I didn't want to argue too much because the Great Entity was so wonderful and so awesome. The love that was emanated was overwhelming.

But there was one more problem, one that seemed unbearable to contemplate. "The reason I can't go back," I said, "is because I can't bear to be away from you anymore." They said, "You won't be away from us. We're with you. We've always been with you. We always will be right with you all the time." I said, "But how do I know that? You tell me that, but when I go back there it's just going to be a nice theory." They said, "Any time you need us we'll be there for you." I said, "You mean like you'll just appear." They said, "No, no. We're not going to intervene in your life in any big way unless you need us. We're just going to be there and you'll feel our presence, you'll feel our love." I said, "If you promise that I can touch your love and if your love can touch me when I need it, I could make it back there. I could do it." They said, "Are you aready?" With no sense of transition whatsoever, I was immediately back in my body in the Paris hospital.

Return to life wasn't easy for Howard. In addition to his physical problems, he had to face the usual array of uncomprehending and insensitive responses to his new spiritual condition. I asked Howard, on the phone, to discuss his difficulties and coping skills.

It began in the hospital, he said. I felt this overwhelming sense of love for everyone. I wanted to hug and kiss everyone, but I couldn't even sit up. I would say, "Oh you're so beautiful" to anyone and everyone. I was the joke of the floor. People found it very amusing.

This went on for several months. I would hug people, and they misunderstood. They thought I was a "lech." I discovered there were a whole bunch of people who didn't want it, so I tried to be real selective about whom I hugged. I asked Howard if he had stopped hugging. He said, "No, I would rather keep trying to share this love I feel and look foolish."

Like other NDErs, Howard's sense of empathy expanded, as well as his compassion. He told me that he initially felt as though he were on an emotional roller coaster. He could, he said, feel the emotions of others more powerfully than his own. For example, he said, I was at a faculty meeting that erupted into a brawl. Everyone was swearing, and I sat there with my hands over my head. I could feel their hurt and anger, and I was praying. Someone said, "Oh, you think you're too good for us do you?" I just said, "I've got a headache." It was a lie, but I felt I had to say that. I "translate" a lot.

Howard's still keen social sense helped him adjust. "I found the emotional roller coaster socially embarrassing," he said. "Someone would talk about a beautiful sunrise, and I would begin to cry. I had to desensitize, so I created a defensive crust. Now I can watch TV and I'm indifferent. The 'crust' has, unfortunately become my reality again."

Howard says that his new interest in philosophy was also socially embarrassing. The world had a "surreal" quality because he was now aware of the other level that existed behind it. When he tried to talk to people about it they either appeared unwilling or unable to connect to this other reality.

"I read a lot," he told me. "I was reading good stuff: Merton, Chardin, and others. Without sounding egotistical, I knew what they knew and sometimes more. I had the feeling sometimes that they were hiding what they really knew. Anyway, I was just barely coping when I met Scott Quimby.

"About nine months after my NDE, Scott was looking for a real live NDEr to interview, and I needed someone to talk to. It was love at first sight. He was trained in psychology and asked good questions; but mostly he just listened, which was exactly what I needed." When I asked if Scott had changed as a result of their relationship, Howard said yes. Scott had begun the relationship as an agnostic but was now a "theist" though he wasn't sure what kind.

I asked Howard what else had helped. He said time and talking. "I have an opportunity to talk to a lot of groups about my NDE," he told me, "and I find that incredibly freeing. I've met people who haven't talked about their NDE for thirty-five years, and it feels to me like they're about to have a psychotic break."

Howard continues to work on his spiritual growth as well as return to life. He says his greatest struggle is to remain humble, and not to let his ego become too big. Before his experience, Howard told me, he was extremely egotistical and controlling. Now he wants a healthy ego, which he describes as a kind of mental pattern, that is under his control. Howard and I shared the sense that these struggles are never finished, though there may be momentary plateaus.

The struggle in the Storm household has, however, subsided. Initially, Howard says, he was alienated from his family. "They simply didn't believe me. So I entered my most destructive, Bible-thumping period. I kept quoting Scripture at them. I thought, if you don't believe me, maybe you'll believe this. Here it is, it says the same thing here." Unfortunately for Howard, his family were agnostic, and Scripture did not carry the seal of approval. On the contrary, one night about two in the morning his wife threatened to leave him. "I love you," she said, "but I can't stand you." "I couldn't believe what I was hearing," said Howard. "I thought I was doing her the biggest favor in the world, trying to get her to believe the great stuff I had learned in my NDE, and she was going to leave. I had been heaping her with verbal abuse, however, and I agreed to be quiet." "After all," she said, "I am right for me."

Howard, like many NDErs, had to relearn respect for the world as it was when he left it. That was a difficult task. On return, he felt his wife's job as an attorney was "nothing but dog food." Howard had begun seminary, and plans to enter the ministry, but even he laughs as he realizes that it looks foolish in the world's scheme of things. His wife approves of his decision. They have no financial concerns, and Howard has agreed not to let his new career interfere with their relationship. The reassurance that the relationship, however strained, will remain intact is, as I said, the bottom line. Peace has come to the Storm household.

Howard decided to enter the Christian ministry after his NDE, but he doesn't believe that Christianity is the only important religion. It was, he said, culturally perfect for me. I think if I had been a Hindu, let's say, I would have seen a Hindu God. If God respects me, which He does, then He respects my culture. I try not to impose my Christianity on other people, he told me. If people have God-like characteristics, a feeling of compassion and living that out, then its OK. I respond more to behavior than philosophy. God really doesn't care a fig about theology.

I asked Howard if he ever thought of entering a monastery. He laughed and said, "Yes, I wondered what it would feel like to be Brother Howard." He visited one, and when he returned his wife said she thought he wouldn't be coming back. His friends, however, admonished him about his responsibilities to his family. Howard agrees they are equally important and has designed his life as a compromise between his family and vocation.

Howard's recovery has been, from my experience, remarkable. He is warm, humble, intelligent and balanced. He had, however, a number of advantages. He encountered, early, a positive significant person in Scott Quimby. Howard had also acquired intelligence and maturity prior to his NDE. Often it is what we bring to the NDE that determines its outcome, as well as what we learn in "heaven" and what we do with it upon return.

Chapter 4

The Near-Death Experience

Howard, Grace and Dianne are not alone. A 1981 Gallup poll estimated that about five percent of the American population, or roughly twelve million people have had a near-death experience (NDE). Thirty-five to forty percent of those resuscitated from clinical death report a sequence of events — discovering themselves outside their physical bodies watching resuscitation attempts; moving through a dark tunnel; entering a heavenly or paradisal realm; or encountering a Being of Light who radiates unconditional love, total knowledge, and all the power of the Universe. Upon return, near-death experiencers (NDErs) discover they have changed in significant ways, and need to learn to live all over again.

This ancient phenomenon has an equally interesting recent history. Raymond Moody's book *Life After Life*, published in 1976, became a surprise bestseller and spawned continuing near-death research and public debate. Its bestseller status is a measure of the public's hunger to hear more about an experience which had become a taboo. Like Elizabeth Kubler-Ross's work on the taboo topic of death, Moody made it permissible to speak about the NDE.

Moody's book aroused the research interest of two disparate scientists, humanistic psychologist Kenneth Ring and physician Michael Sabom. Ring decided to quantify Moody's essentially anecdotal report, and published his findings in the book *Life at Death*.

Sabom was working separately on his own research. Originally a skeptic, Sabom began his research on a dare, and ended a believer. Sabom concentrated on the out-of-body phase of the NDE, intent on disproving the out-of-body (OBE) experience by checking accounts of those purporting to have left their bodies, against the facts. Instead he proved the impossible. He had to concede that it was unlikely that detailed accounts of resuscitation attempts, down to verbatim conversations and minute details of dress, had been fabricated. Description of details outside the hospital room could probably be attributed to an OBE journey during resuscitation, as described by his patients. Sabom's so-called veridical proof of OBE information continues to confound skeptics.

Together Ring and Sabom began to place the NDE on a solid statistical foundation. They discovered that it was far more common than had previously been supposed, and that there were enough common features (the so-called invariance hypothesis) to call the complete phenomenon the near-death experience.

New discoveries were to follow in simultaneous publications by psychologists Margot Grey and Ring. They had found the aftereffects, those transformative changes that accompany an NDE. Eager to offer explanations, Ring proposed the kundalini hypothesis and the concept of the evolution of consciousness. They both agreed that the NDE was a spontaneous spiritual experience, or an initial (or initiatory) mystical experience. Grey concluded thoughtfully that the NDE was not automatically transformative.

Much later and more slowly came the discoveries of the difficulties accompanying reentry, or return to life. These have received only tentative treatment, so far, in the near-death literature. *Coming Back Again* by PMH Atwater openly discusses some of these difficulties in a personal and colloquial fashion. Other references to problems and counseling suggestions are found scattered throughout the near-death literature and random journal articles.

Theologians have been as tardy as therapists to examine the NDE. Dr. Carol Zalesky of the Department of Religious Studies of Harvard University, while not a theologian, offers splendid though limited religious insight. In her book *Otherworld Journeys* she compares medieval and modern near-death accounts, and provides an intellectual analysis of the contemporary near-death scene. Her explanation of the NDE as symbolic narrative is meant to mediate between the skeptics and naive believers.

Scientific near-death research was not to end with the initial publications by Moody, Ring and Sabom. Psychiatrist Dr. Bruce Greyson publishes extensively in medical journals and specializes in near-death experiences that have resulted from suicide attempts. Contrary to previous opinion, suicides do not go straight to hell and do have positive NDEs.

Ring, Moody and Greyson became confederates in an important new venture, the founding of the International Association of Near Death Studies (IANDS). IANDS supports a data bank, sponsors research and a yearly international near-death conference, publishes a journal and informal newsletter, and founded Friends of IANDS, an international network of near-death support groups. The work of IANDS has contributed to near-death credibility, gained media attention for the experience, and served as personal savior to many NDErs.

What is this experience that has aroused the ire and imagination of so many? Moody, Ring and Sabom each devised schemes for organizing the disparate elements of the NDE. Moody noticed a continuity of discrete elements, such as buzzing noises, encounters with spiritual beings, a border, etc. and organized the NDE around fifteen core elements. Sabom differentiated between the "autoscopic" or OBE and transcedent stages, beyond the tunnel. Ring devised a five-phase scheme, later amended to include the Light. I have used Ring's scheme since it can be compared with both Universal and Christian stages of spiritual development. The implication drawn from this is that at each near-death phase a higher level of physical consciousness has been achieved. Indeed fewer and fewer individuals recount deep stages of the NDE, as few individuals attain the highest stages of mystical awareness.

As the NDE occurs outside of time and space, the phase model is imposed on a simultaneous experience. Phases may be skipped, but the order of phases appears to be irreversible. Each phase has its own unique experiences which may startle the uninformed and inexperienced. Consequently, the phases will be described in detail using stories from the existing near-death literature as well as my personal interviews and experience. By using many researchers, I have corrected for skewed findings and biased reporting, though I have undoubtedly added my own.

After describing the five phases of peace, OBE, tunnel, heaven or paradise, and the Light, I will discuss the morally important life-review, hellish experiences and prophetic visions. I will also add a discovery of my own, the existence of a deep near-death phase I call the Darkness of God.

Early research focused on the Light as Deity to the exclusion of the Darkness of God. Later research disclosed that the light appeared in several forms: as the light that illuminated heaven, single and individual spiritual beings of light, and the Light itself, or the Being of Light. Closer inspection of the experiences of darkness disclose similar nuances. Darkness may be used to describe hell, the transitional tunnel and the Void or Formlessness which I call the Darkness of God.

Here in the West we value something over nothing. We value forms and images and endow them with more reality than the emptiness perceived in the East as Ultimate Reality. This bias has no doubt blinded near-death researchers to the meaning and nuances of darkness. The few dark experiences reported in the literature, called "non experiences," may constitute the last and deepest phase of the NDE.

To draw or describe an event occurring outside of this world of time and space is difficult. NDErs often struggle for words. The experience is ineffable. Nonetheless, some NDErs are eloquent. It is the most wonderful thing that ever happened to them, and many long to share it at length. The cumulative impact of millions of credible witnesses is, I find, convincing.

Phase One — Peace and Contentment

"I had a feeling of total peace. A feeling of total, total peace... It was just such a total peaceful sensation...I wasn't frightened anymore."

To describe the near-death experience, others use words like "euphoric" or "orgasmic" or "It felt like when you wake up in the morning and you feel real good."

For some the near-death experience terminates at this phase. For others, the good feelings predominate throughout the remainder of the NDE.

Phase Two — Out-of-Body

> I was in the intensive care unit of Worthing Hospital. During the early hours, I found myself suspended above my body looking down at myself. I heard and saw two doctors and a nurse running towards the bed and heard them say "quick, quick." I am sure I had died.

This brief out-of-body description, similar to Dianne's introduces the near-death experience, for which the stage of peace and contentment act as preliminary. Experiencer reactions range from feelings of naturalness or euphoria, to more negative emotions of fear or panic. "Many people find the notion of being out of their body so unthinkable that, even as they are experiencing it, they feel conceptually quite confused about the whole thing."

> In a complete out-of-body phase, experiencers: . . . Typically . . . tended to find themselves in the room above the body, often in a corner, looking down at their prostrate form as if they were a spectator. They usually state that at the time this seemed quite natural, and also report a heightened but detached mental process, more acute hearing, and a very brightly illuminated environment. This situation is described as being distinctly real. They feel as much alive as before, in fact many of the respondents reported feeling more alive and were conscious of everything that was happening. During this period the individual can be observed to have reached the stage of brain death, with complete cessation of neurological function, deep unconsciousness without response to painful stimuli and without any EEG electrical activity.

While the clinically dead physical body lies on a hospital table, the near-death experiencer feels himself to be elsewhere: "I felt like I was up near the light, on the ceiling, or something looking down," or even "I seemed to be higher than the ceiling."

> The author of *I Died Three Times in 1977* found herself floating up to the ceiling, looking down at her motionless frame. "When I was satisfied that I was dead, there came a joyous euphoria, like a prisoner being released from a long jail sentence. I danced and danced around the light bulb, singing like a child. It was finally over, I was free."

NDErs are often merely aware that "they" are somewhere other than in their physical body:

> I was *above*. I don't know above what. But I was (pause) up...it was like (pause) like I didn't have a body! I was (pause) but it was me. Not a body, but me! You know what I mean?... It was me inside. The real me was up there; not this here (pointing to her physical body).

While some correlate this new identity with "consciousness" others reported having a "new body." In Ring's study, thirty-seven percent entered phase two, but only one reported having another body. Moody, on the other hand, encountered only one or two cases who felt they were disembodied: "They felt as though they were 'pure' consciousness."

NDErs often have difficulty describing this new body. The ineffability of the near-death experience extends to the out-of-body, as well as later phases. However, "words and phrases which have been used by various subjects include a mist, a cloud, wispy, an energy pattern and others which express similar meanings." One of the five cases described by Moody will serve as representative of the sample:

> I lost control of my car on a curve... At that point, I kind of lost my sense of time, and I lost my physical reality as far as my body is concerned — I lost touch with my body. My being or my self or my spirit, or whatever you would like to label it — I could sort of feel it rise out of me, out through my head. And it wasn't anything that hurt, it was just sort of like lifting and it was being above me...(My being) felt as if it had *density* to it, almost, but not a physical density — kind of like, I don't know, waves or something, I guess. Nothing really physical, almost as if it were charged, if you'd like to call it that. But it felt as if it had something to it...It was small, and it felt as if it were sort of circular, with no rigid outlines to it. You could liken it to an encasement...

The state of being in this new body is different from being in a physical body. There are limitations. NDErs are unable to communicate with those around them either through speech or touch. "People were walking from all directions to get to the wreck...As they came real close, I would try to turn around, to get out of their way, but they would just walk *through* me."

In addition to the negative emotions related above, the inability to communicate causes some to feel isolated and lonely.

> I was unable to touch anything, unable to communicate with any of the people around. It is an awesome, lonely feeling, a feeling of complete isolation. I knew that I was completely alone, by myself.

Others experienced this state as pleasant, natural, even euphoric. There are new freedoms to compensate for the limitations.

> Travel, once one gets the hang of it, is apparently exceptionally easy. Physical objects present no barrier, and movement from one place to another can be extremely rapid, almost instantaneous.

A sense of timelessness and spacelessness pervade this phase. New mental and visual acuity are also acquired.

> Things that are not possible now, are then. Your mind is so clear. It's so nice. My mind just took down everything and worked everything out for me the first time, without having to go through it more than once. After a while everything I was experiencing got to where it meant something to me in some way.

One man says that while he was "dead" his vision seemed incredibly more powerful and in his words, "I just can't understand how I could see so far." A woman who recalled this experience notes, "It seemed as if this spiritual sense had no limitations, as if I could look everywhere."

Other sensory experience is absent or rare. The sense of hearing is often replaced by telepathic communication:

> I could see people all around, and I could understand what they were saying. I didn't hear them audibly, like I'm hearing you. It was more like knowing what they were thinking, exactly what they were thinking, but only in my mind, not in their actual vocabulary. I would catch it the second before they opened their mouths to speak."

The OBE phase of the NDE ends either with return to the physical body or to a deeper, more profound near-death experience.

> Then I heard a voice, it was not an English voice, but it sounded foreign saying "Margaret, go back, go back." I next felt as if a blind was pulled down and I shot back into my conscious state and woke up in the hospital bed.

For others, the temporary state of loneliness caused by the inability to contact living loved ones is dispelled as they are greeted by deceased loved ones, spiritual beings, or the Being of Light.

The OBE is neither specific to the NDE, nor need it be mystical or spiritual. However, the discovery that life does not end with physical death, and that one's essential identity is "soul," "spirit," or "consciousness" may precipitate a spiritual conversion, and a conscious search for higher mystical states.

The possibility that we can leave our bodies is inconceivable to those who have not experienced it. However, not only is it possible to leave our bodies behind when we die, we frequently do so at other times as well. Melodie Olson, RN, provides a clinical definition of an out-of-body state in her article, "The Incidence of Out-of-Body Experiences in Hospitalized Patients," in the Spring 1988 issue of the *Journal of Near Death Studies*:

> When a person feels his or her mind, consciousness, or center of aware-
> ness to be at a place different from the physical body. It is different from
> a hallucination or schizophrenic loss of body boundaries in that the person
> seems well based on other mental health parameters. It is different from
> depersonalization in that it is not accompanied by extreme anxiety, but is
> calming and satisfying . . . (And it) is not a dream, but is much more realistic
> than even vivid dreams, and frequently occurs while awake.

The cultural concensus that such states are impossible is a symptom of the materialistic mind-set that believes that life ends with physical death. If we are only bodies, then death means personal annihilation.

Theology and pastoral care have become secular insofar as they refuse to accept the reality of the non-material substance of soul or spirit. The actual experiences, by credible witnesses, of these immaterial or spiritual entities may encourage theologians, pastors and clinicians to again take these aspects of the human psyche seriously.

Phase Three — The Dark Tunnel

Phase three marks the transition between the paranormal OBE phase and the supernormal stages which follow. Such transitional stages accompany other altered states of consciousness, and are not specific to the NDE.

In the tunnel experience NDErs recall:

> . . . Going through a tunnel, a very, very dark tunnel . . . It started at a
> narrow point and became wider and wider. But I remember it being very,
> very black. But even though it was black, I wasn't afraid because I knew
> that there was something at the other end waiting for me that was good . . .

My experience of darkness has enabled me to distinguish nuances of dark-
ness missed by other researchers. Together with the tunnel, hell is also described as dark, as are other experiences which I call the Darkness of God, as in the case of John Wren-Lewis of the Department of Religious Studies, University of Sydney, Australia. Upon return from death, Wren-Lewis relates the attempt at recall resulted in a "recognition of the deepest darkness I had

ever known, which was somehow right behind my eyes." This darkness was peaceful and secure. Wren-Lewis describes this darkness with analogies from poetry and the world's religious traditions as a "dazzling or shining dark," the "living Void" of Taoism, Hinduism, Tibetan Buddhism and Zen; Meister Eckhart's description of the Godhead as "empty though it were not," and Jacob Boehme's reference to God as a "supersensual abyss."

> In the creation story of the Maoris of New Zealand it is said that "in the beginning there was 'Te Kore,' the Nothing. . . and into the void of nothing-ness and night came a gleam of light, a speck of light. Light unseen for there was none to see. . . ." To coin my own phrase, it was as if the personal "I" budded out from that eternity of shining dark, without my ceasing to be the shining dark. . . And the whole process was blissful, which is another marked contrast between my experience and a great many near-death experiences. There was no sense of regret at coming back from the heavenly state or "place" into the narrow world of physical existence. Manifestation seemed to be just another mode, as it were of the bliss of the Unmanifest.

With a little effort Wren-Lewis was able to maintain that awareness in the midst of life:

> At first in Thailand, I again and again caught myself thinking, "Oh, God, it's gone" — but then, as soon as I focused on the fact that I was missing something from my life, it all came flooding back, with no effort on my part at all, the shining dark void at the back of my head and behind every-thing else, and the experience of everything coming freshly into glorious existence now! now! and now!

Wren-Lewis is not alone. Like Dianne, others describe the dark as ". . . just like a void, nothing and it's. . . (so) peaceful. . . ." Or, "It was empty, yeah, that's it. Space. Just nothing, nothing but something. It's like trying to describe the end of the universe," and "My happiness had no connection with the fact that I was alive again; my happiness seemed at that time to be connected with that total peaceful blackness."

The comparison of phases of the NDE with Universal stages of mystical consciousness presented in the chapter on mysticism suggests that Wren-Lewis' experience of darkness belongs at the last phase of the NDE; either together with the light in the paradoxical coincidence of opposites which char-acterizes higher mystical consciousness, or as a separate and later stage.

Phase Four — Entering the World of Light or Paradise.

"It was dark and it was like — hard to believe — like you were going from dark to light. I can't explain it. . . all of a sudden there was light. . . ."

In the transition from darkness to light, one-fifth of Ring's subjects entered a world of light, or a paradisial realm. Descriptions of the world of light or paradise include references to preternaturally beautiful landscapes, ethereal music, meeting deceased relatives or spiritual beings. These "motifs of paradise" are described as:

> . . .A trip to heaven. I saw the most beautiful lakes. Angels, they were floating around like you see seagulls. Everything was white. The most beautiful flowers. Nobody on this earth ever saw the beautiful flowers that I saw there. . .I don't believe there is a color on this earth that wasn't included in that color situation that I saw. Everything, everything. Of course, I was so impressed with the beauty of everything there that I couldn't pinpoint any one thing. . .Everything was bright. The lakes were blue, light blue. Everything about the angels was pure white.

> And there was music, very, very pleasant music. . .The music was beautiful. . .And then there was another part to it where two aunts of mine, they're dead. . .they started calling to me.

> Suddenly there was this tremendous burst of light and, uh, I was turned to the light. I saw at a great distance a city. . .and. . .the light was coming from within this city. The first thing that I saw was this street. And it had such clarity. The only thing that I can relate it to in this light was a look of gold, but it was clear, it was transparent. . .Everything there had a purity and clarity. . .The flowers and the flower buds by that street — the intensity, the vibrant colors, like pebbles that have been polished in a running stream, but they were all like precious stones, rubies and diamonds and sapphires.

Return from this phase is facilitated by a deceased relative or spirit guide who warns the individual that it is not time to die. A "border" which blocks entry into death may also be encountered.

> Yet it wasn't my time to go through the mist, because instantly from the other side appeared my Uncle Carl, who had died many years earlier. He blocked my path saying, "Go back. Your work on earth has not been completed. Go back now." I didn't want to go back but I had no choice, and immediately I was back in my body.

Grace, too, had a heavenly or paradisial NDE, though she found herself on the wrong side of the mist and had to recross to life. Apparently, she did have a choice, however, and was guided in making her decision by her Lord.

Drawn back to earth by the love and/or need of living relatives or some unfinished work, NDErs are nevertheless reluctant to leave heaven. "Why, in heaven's name, did you bring me back? It was so beautiful."

Phase Five — Encountering the Light, or The Being of Light.

Encounter with the Light, or Being of Light is described as "the most incredible common element in the accounts" and the event which "has the most profound effect upon the individual." Ring, in *Heading Toward Omega*, terms the encounter with the Light a "full" or "particularly deep" NDE. The Light is described as Personal, but not a person;

> The next sensation is this wonderful, wonderful feeling of this light...It's almost like a person. It is not a person, but it is a being of some kind. It is a mass of energy. It doesn't have a character like you would describe another person, but it has a character in that it is more than just a thing. And also in size, it just covers the entire vista before you. And it totally engulfs whatever the horizon might be...

The same NDEr, Tom Sawyer, describes two outstanding features of the Light — perfect love and total knowledge.

> Then the thing is, the light communicates to you and for the first time in your life...it is a feeling of true, pure love...The second most magnificent experience...is that you are suddenly in communication with absolute, total knowledge...

Communication with the Light is telepathic. "It's absolutely instant, absolutely clear. It wouldn't even matter if a different language was being spoken..."

The Light telepathically asks questions such as, "Are you prepared to die?" "Are you ready to die?" "What have you done with your life to show me?" and "What have you done with your life that is sufficient?" All are spoken in a tone of total love and acceptance.

The Light also answers questions. "You can think a question...and immediately know the answer to it...And it can be any question whatsoever. It can be on any subject..."

Entering or merging with the Light can be part of the experience.

> It was total immersion in light, brightness, warmth, peace, security. I did not have an out-of-body experience. I just went immediately into this beautiful light. It's difficult to describe; as a matter of fact, it's impossible to describe. Verbally, it cannot be expressed. It's something which becomes you and you become it. I could say, "I was peace, I was love." I was the brightness, it was a part of me...you just know. You're all-knowing — and everything is a part of you — it's — it's just so beautiful. It was eternity. It's like I was always there and I will always be there, and that my existence on earth was just a brief instant.

Return from this phase, unlike return from Paradise, is voluntary. The Light provides NDErs with a choice to stay or return. All who come back say their return was due to unfinished business, or to the pull of loved ones. But those who have reached the light are often as reluctant as the heavenly citizen to return: "I never wanted to leave the presence of this being." All do return, however, having completed their NDE, only to be greeted by a reluctant world and a difficult period of recovery.

Prophetic Visions

Like Grace and Howard, panoramic visions of the future, referred to as "Prophetic Visions," were encountered by others in the full or deep NDE. The following example is characteristic:

> The vision of the future I received during my near-death experience was one of tremendous upheaval in the world as a result of our general ignorance of the "true" reality. I was informed that mankind was breaking the laws of the universe and as a result of this would suffer. The suffering was not due to the vengeance of an indignant God but rather like the pain one might suffer as a result of arrogantly defying the law of gravity. It was to be an inevitable educational cleansing of the earth that would creep up upon its inhabitants, who would try to hide blindly in institutions of law, science, and religion. Mankind, I was told, was being consumed by the cancers of arrogance, materialism, racism, chauvinism, and separatist thinking. I saw sense turning to nonsense, and calamity, in the end, turning to providence. At the end of this general period of transition, mankind was to be "born anew" with a new sense of his place in the universe. The birth process, however, as in all the kingdoms, was exquisitely painful. Mankind would emerge humbled, yet educated, peaceful, and at last unified.

Life Review

The life review, or a moment in which one's whole life flashes before one, can happen at any time during the NDE. Like Frank, below, those whose life review proceeds under the gaze of the Being of Light and Love, however, feel a sense of forgiveness rather than guilt or punishment.

> It was like I got to view my whole life as a movie, and see it and get to view different things that happened, different things that took place. I think I got to see some things in the future. I might even have gotten to see how my whole life might have turned out. . . And the next thing was a voice coming to me . . . and saying very compassionately. . . ."You really

blew it this time Frank." . . . It was like, I have a mission here to do, let's say, and I had a choice of what basically I call going on with the physical body or starting over again with a new one. . . I don't know if I actually did see all of my life — that's too hard to say — but I remember it was like going to certain little things. Some of them seemed very insignificant. . . you wouldn't think that they had any significance in your life. . . It was like I got to see some good things I had done and some mistakes I had made, and you try to understand them. It was like: "Okay, here's why you had the accident. Here's why this happened.". . . It all had meaning. There was no feeling of guilt. It was all right.

Under the loving gaze of the Light NDErs learn what is important and what is not. One NDEr relates that:

I was asked — "What had I done to benefit the human race?" At the same time my life was presented instantly in front of me and I was shown what counted. I am not going into this any further, but, believe me, what I had counted in life as unimportant was my salvation, and what I thought was important was nil.

And another one discovered:

Somehow we have a more important mission while we're here. Okay. That's it. We have a more important mission in our lives than just the material end of it in trying just to get material gains. There are more important things. It showed that. . . love is important and that every human being on earth is just as equal to each other. They are all the same. It sort of brought that aspect out in my life. I don't know. It's something I wasn't too aware of before. Before I had a lot more prejudice.

The purposefulness of life is stressed equally with love. "The voice asked me a question: 'Is it worth it?' And what it meant was, did the kind of life I had been leading up to that point seem worthwhile to me, knowing what I knew then."

The idea of sin as we've come to accept it is changed for the NDEr:

And I said to him, this is all so beautiful, this is all so perfect, what about my sins? And he said to me, there are no sins. Not in the way you think about them on earth. The only thing that matters here is how you think. "What is in your heart?" He asked me — and I saw there was nothing in my heart except love. . .

While there is no sin in the sense of multiple transgressions, there are prohibitions.

(While I was over there) I got the feeling that two things it was completely forbidden for me to do would be to kill myself or to kill another person . . . If I were to commit suicide, I would be interfering with God's purpose for the individual.

God is no longer a stern and condemning judge, but loving, forgiving and accepting. Nevertheless, there is discrimination between right and wrong. A single prohibition replaces the ten — it is wrong to kill; and a positive injunction given — to love. Priorities are rearranged, new guidelines given for life. The individual is forgiven, cleansed and given a fresh start.

You are judging yourself. You have been forgiven all your sins, but are you able to forgive yourself for doing the things you shouldn't have done? Some little cheaty things that maybe you've done in life? Can you forgive yourself? This is the judgment . . .

Hell

The popular image of the NDE is one of heavenly bliss and light. However, there are hellish experiences.

I felt an inner struggle going on between myself and some evil force. At the last moment I suddenly felt an inner explosion and seemed to be enveloped in a blue flame which felt cold. At this point I found myself floating about six inches above my body. The next thing I remember is being sucked down a vast black vortex like a whirlpool and I found myself in a place that I can only describe as being like Dante's Inferno. I saw a lot of other people who seemed grey and dreary and there was a musty smell of decay. There was an overwhelming feeling of loneliness about the place.

Though few hellish experiences have been recorded, the existence of hellish experiences suggests that possibility for any of us. Though as a society we are growing in love and light, we do not like to think we will be ultimately accountable for our actions and attitudes. The NDE suggests otherwise. Whether to hell or heaven, amendment of life is the outcome of the near-death adventure.

Interpretation

The NDE has been described in detail, but what are we to make of it, what is it, what does it mean, and who has one? According to Ring, the NDE correlates with no known demographic variables such as age, sex, religion or geographic region. Even self-styled atheists and children have NDEs. The few cross cultural studies that exist suggest some culturally determined differences within a universal core experience.

Physical interpretations search for causes in physical functions such as oxygen deprivation, anesthesia, endorphins and so forth. Attempts to find physical causes have been unsuccessful so far.

In the physical interpretation, no meaning is given the NDE beyond pathological mental or physical activity, and the common interpretation is "hallucination." The scientific skeptic has difficulty conceiving of a reality beyond the material realm and dismisses the NDE as impossible or pathological.

Others have interpreted the NDE as a mystical experience. Those who do have little difficulty conceiving of a reality beyond the physical, and respect and affirm the possibility of mystical experience. It is not impossible for them to envision an immaterial entity of soul or spirit; and it is a joy rather than a disgrace to discover that life may persist beyond bodily death.

Broad-minded and intelligent believers continue to collect near-death data and search for physical correlates, not causes, to increase our understanding of the NDE. Others seek to penetrate more deeply into the meaning of mysticism. We believe that the meaning of the NDE can be found in the essence and nature of life itself — that we are spiritual as well as physical beings with a basic drive to rediscover God.

Chapter 5

Aftereffects of the Near-Death Experience

"It ain't over til it's over" NDErs discover as they return from death to a new self and an often alien world. In time, NDErs and researchers became aware of significant and startling changes, called aftereffects, in those who had an NDE. Personalities alter, and families no longer recognize parent or spouse. Identity or sense of self has changed, as has emotional expression, mental content and ability, and the potential for psychic or paranormal perception. A new energy, obtained in the light, inhabits their now relatively unimportant bodies. The energy which often healed them and allows them to heal others, comes in uncontrollable cycles. New gifts are discovered, like the ability to heal, and latent gifts and talents begin to emerge, together with a total change in values, goals, priorities.

Encounter with a loving presence has convinced them of the value of service and the futility of accumulating wealth or competing for status. These "religious" values are enhanced by new knowledge that God exists and the Afterlife is real. Attitudes toward religion become more universal, pluralistic and spiritual. NDErs know that all religions proclaim the same inner core of truth, and all are beautiful. Inner relationship with the divine, however, becomes more important than external worship.

Almost all of these near-death aftereffects can be found in the mystical literature. They are the expected side effects of mystical experience. From the phases of experience and array of aftereffects which are normal for the NDE each individual will exhibit only a few. In general, the deeper the NDE, however, the more profound the change.

"Return from death is a two-edge sword," said one NDEr, for the changes are both transforming and troubling. Even the most transformative changes become troublesome in an unwelcoming world, where the fruits of mystical experience are perceived as signs of insanity. NDErs return to earth with a crash, confused and sad; perplexed and persecuted. They need time and understanding to recover.

Self-Discovery

New norms discovered in heaven or the Light, replace old cultural ones. The deviance of the NDEr is often perceived, however, as "sick" or "wrong" rather than a valued and valid advance in human development.

Humanist psychologist Abraham Maslow discovered signs of healthy growth in people who had had transcendent experiences. The signs include the development of a new and authentic sense of self, new modes of loving and knowing, greater need for solitude, development of latent gifts and talents, a sense of mission or purpose, and values that coincide with the world's religious traditions. NDErs fit that description.

Changes in NDEr sense of self may include a mystical feeling of divine identity. One friend discovered after death that she was a tiny spark of Light. Those that merge with the light feel they have momentarily become the Light. Dianne felt she was the blackness. The most significant near-death change, however, is the discovery of a real and authentic self hidden under layers of defense. Said one woman describing the sensation of "self" during the initial phase of her near-death experience: "For the first time in my life I was completely myself — not anyone's wife or mother." Barbara Harris says:

> I was acting. My whole life was acting because I always had the feeling that if people found out who I really was they wouldn't like me, that I was really very bad. I had walked around for thirty-one years hiding the fact that I was bad. Every time I got spanked, I felt I was bad. And the few times something good happened to me, I was aware, "Well, they don't know the real you." So up until that point in my life it was an act. An act to be good so people would know that I was a good person and if I could win everybody over, then I would finally like myself.
>
> But when I came back from that [her near-death experience], I really understood. I had a real feeling of understanding that I was a good person and all I had to do was be me . . . It was a feeling all of a sudden that if people would get to know the real me . . . that they would have to like me. [And you really did experience the real you in this state, it seems.] Yeah, I knew at that point that I had met myself . . . Without sounding corny, that was the most important incident of my thirty-nine years and the rebirth of who I am now. That was really being born again. I can vividly go back to who I was before that time. I can put myself into that mental state . . . but it's a totally different human being that I am now. If I still had to be that other Barbara, I wouldn't want to be walking around. I would probably find something else that hurt just as badly as my back and I would probably have a tremendous need for all the pain medication and/or drinking and/or pot and/or something to fill that emptiness that was so much a part of me. That experience made me whole and that experience wiped away all the scars that I collected and that experience gave me all the tools to struggle through these seven years and get to the feeling now that I'm always here. You know, it took me a long time to recapture that person. Everybody around me, I felt, was restricting me from becoming that person because of who they were. So the experience itself gave me that spirituality that I needed and the tools that I needed to become who I am now.

Barbara's story was chosen to share at length since she illustrates several aspects of healthy growth. Barbara speaks of a "real" basically good self, hidden under layers of trauma, faulty interpersonal relationships and defenses. She speaks of the years and work necessary to integrate and consolidate this new sense of self.

Barbara's new self-acceptance and authenticity is echoed by another NDEr:

> I think I used to be a very superficial person, always breaking my butt to please or be accepted or to be liked. Now I just don't give a damn anymore. It's really a delicious feeling...

Grace, too, discovered that she was acceptable, and rearranged her priorities. Now, as she says, God comes first, then me and then my husband and kids. Rearranged priorities and newly assertive women can disturb the family *status quo*. Roles change as women who are discovering themselves move into the marketplace, and men quit lucrative jobs to go into the helping professions. The NDE appears to balance the extremes of gender stereotypes. As women become more assertive, men, like Joe Geraci, become more compassionate.

> And I can recall in my attempt to hold onto this feeling and to hold onto this peace, I began to bump into earthly things that you know, of course, aren't going to escape from you — they're there. My first frustrating experience was with the television. I couldn't watch television. There would be a commercial, a cosmetic commercial. I couldn't — I'd have to turn it off because it was something false. It was unnecessary, it was fake. It just didn't belong (it was) insignificant. Any type of violence, if there was even an old Western, an old Western movie, I'd have to turn it off because to me that was total ignorance. There was just no reason on earth to show people killing people. That was frustrating, especially when the family was sitting down trying to watch television and Dad gets up and turns it off all the time! So I finally learned to just go to my room.

New Rules, Values, Goals

Joe illustrates the attitude of those who have had an NDE toward cultural convention — that it is phoney and false. Attachment to human convention is severed together with other ties that bind the NDEr to the human community — emotional ties to family and a shared common language. I can remember at my return how astonished I was to discover, like the Quaker George Fox, that the conventional rules we live by are man-made, unimportant and immaterial. As a result, I, like Joe, gave up caring excessively about my appearance. Joe says he now greets guests at the door in his bathrobe.

Careless attire is an expression of the near-death tendency to de-emphasize body image, like Grace, who thinks now it is the inner soul or self that is important. NDErs have outgrown the need to rely on body image, wealth or status for acceptance. God, not humans, provides their norms for morality and behavior.

God-given values are not the accumulation of wealth or competition for status, but learning to love and discovering purpose, as Joseph Dippong discovered:

> Although this event occurred a long time ago, it marked a very crucial point in my life. I began a new chapter, a chapter which was to continue for the rest of my life. This moment and the following minutes and hours changed my life entirely. I was transformed from a man who was lost and wandering aimlessly, with no goal in life other than a desire for material wealth, to someone who had a deep motivation, a purpose in life, a definite direction, and an overpowering conviction that there would be a reward at the end of life similar to the pot of gold at the end of the rainbow . . . The changes in my life were completely positive. My interest in material wealth and greed for possessions were replaced by a thirst for spiritual understanding and a passionate desire to see world conditions improve.

Dippong is not the only NDEr to return with a sense of mission and a search for purpose. Return by choice from the brink of death is due to unfinished business — the care of loved ones or the completion of an important task. Sense of purpose can be personal or social — why was I born, or what am I to do. Search for meaning and purpose can take years. Mission is accomplished when the NDEr discovers a way to act out in service the unconditional love of the Light.

Service may be performed behind the scene in the helping professions or in the limelight of the near-death lecture circuit. In each case the NDEr will encounter conflict: with institutional norms or an envious, incredulous, angry, fearful or adoring public.

Emotions

The NDE appears often to unblock and expand emotional expression. NDErs cry more easily, get angry more often and love with passionate compassion, as Tom Sawyer discovered.

> Then the thing the light communicates to you for the first time in your life — is a feeling of absolute, pure love . . . It can't be compared to the love of your wife, the love of your children, or some people consider

a very intense sexual experience as love and they consider [it] possibly the most beautiful moment in their life — and it couldn't even begin to compare. All of these wonderful, wonderful feelings combined could not possibly compare to the feeling, the true love. . . Upon entering that — Its total love, total knowledge.

Tom Sawyer discovered a new definition and expression of love. Love, the NDEr discovers, is not based on need or dependency; not expressed by desiring or belonging to an exclusive relationship. True love is compassionate, empathic and expressed equally to everyone. St. John of the Cross calls it a spiritual friendship for all.

This love that Maslow calls healthy Being Love envisions the perfection in the beloved, fosters growth of the authentic self of the other, and doesn't cling or control. The leap of love, perhaps the greatest treasure of the NDE, can cause the most unhappiness with spouses who neither want nor understand this other unfamiliar love.

Tom loves more freely and also weeps more easily. Early in his career as a near-death lecturer, Tom wept uncontrollably when he spoke of the Light. He is not alone. Raymond Moody discovered that men were more reticent than women to share their experience because the emotions were so overwhelming they broke down and cried.

Despite the overwhelming love, NDErs may be initially angry as well. Dianne was angry at God for deserting her and forcing her to return to an imperfect world and a painful body. Grace is angry more often now at aggression, injustice and oppression. All can legitimately be angry at the world's hostile reception. Persecution can cause paranoia.

Mental Transformation

Uncomfortable emotional changes are not nearly as disquieting as the mental transformation that accompanies the NDE. Ordinary individuals are transformed by their tour of heaven into citizens of another world. Perception by non-physical senses begun in the NDE and perception of the dead and spiritual beings may persist. They have become psychic seers, and telepathic "knowers." The sudden acquisition of psychic abilities following a near-death experience can be disturbing or devastating as Georgia discovered:

When I woke up and looked around, I can remember knowing everything. And that was the hardest thing. . . (What exactly did you know?) I knew what you were thinking, I knew who was coming into the room. I knew there was someone coming up the hall, and I knew what they were going to say; and before you turned on the radio, I knew what was going to be played. But I didn't tell anyone and I thought, "I have to try to eliminate this: this has to get out of my head!. . ." So anyway, that took a long time to fade.

Touching higher consciousness has radically altered the way they know as well as what they know. They have had a radical mind change, that has taken them outside the confines of ordinary consciousness. The result is a reversal of world-view from that of the average earth-bound individual.

NDErs know new things in a new way. The heavenly phase can result in entering a city of knowledge like one NDEr who says, "Now this cathedral was literally built of knowledge. This was a place of learning I had come to — cause literally all information — I began to be bombarded with data."

Merger with the Light results in the acquisition of whole truths rather than individual bits of information, as Carol Parrish-Harra discovered:

> The Light Being, pure, powerful, all-expansive, was without form and it could be said that great waves of awareness flowed to me and into my mind. . .It seemed whole Truths revealed themselves to me. Waves of thought — ideas greater and purer than I had ever tried to figure out came to me. Thoughts, clear without effort revealed themselves in total wholeness, although not in logical sequence.

The vision of the interconnectedness of all knowledge and all life that characterizes many NDErs is a reflection of the high mystical state of unity consciousness. NDErs have experienced the essential oneness of Being — of all life, knowledge and religions.

NDErs know new information and truths in these new ways; as psychic bits of information or whole and inter-connected mystical "truths." During the life-review NDErs may review past lives, other reincarnations and behold their own future as well as see prophetic visions of the future of the world. Often they discourse with the Being of Light and discover insights into their personal lives and the nature of the physical world, the nature of God and the manner of creation, as did the mystics.

Not all of the insight and information is retained on return to life. Often only vague truths remain, or bits and pieces, glimmers of a higher consciousness, that need to be understood like pieces in a puzzle.

Some continue to be bombarded with psychically clairvoyant knowledge of global and personal catastrophe. Others are able to read the hearts and souls of men and women, and find this an aid in the helping professions. Still others get unsought information about physical phenomena or the nature of creation. For example, Tom Sawyer began to receive Greek symbols and went to the library to find out what they meant. They were physics formulae.

Neither reception nor communication of these truths is easy...NDErs often hear without words, or receive impressions or images that must be translated into language.

> INTERVIEWER: When you heard the voice...did you actually hear the words...? RESPONDENT: It was like it was coming into my mind. It was like I didn't have any hearing or any sight or anything. It was like it was projected into my mind. It was mostly thoughts. It was like — the more I think it over, the more it comes out as words, but when it happened it was more like symbols — symbolic, you know? INTERVIEWER: so what you're doing now is trying to translate it into words? RESPONDENT: I'm trying to change it into English...

Those who have had an NDE tend to think now in symbols, rather than in the linear, literal thought common to our culture. They have activated the right brain, accessed higher more wholistic modes of consciousness, and often momentarily lost their capacity to use ordinary language. They may need to relearn linear, discursive language skills to complement their newly acquired symbolic and poetic style.

Difficulty in understanding and translating is compounded by the inadequacy of earthly language to describe a spiritual world. Three NDErs express this difficulty:

> There are not words...It can't be conveyed. And it cannot be fully understood.
> Yeah, it was like — it was such — I've never had an experience like this. I mean, there's like no, no words to convey.
> This was different from a dream. And different than being on this physical planet. So it was something other than (pause) than what words can express on this planet for sure.

The NDEr, like the poet and other mystics, is reduced to metaphor to describe a real but different world. A communication gap exists between speaker and listener when descriptions of the otherworld are reduced to concrete earthly realities. The experiencer struggles to speak. It is equally important that we struggle to hear, however imperfectly, their message of a more perfect world.

In Howard's more perfect world to come, communication will be telepathic, as it was with the Light. Telepathy may continue now as the communication mode between those who share a similar consciousness. Others, like Howard, do not trust enough to seek telepathic union. Ours is still an imperfect world.

A New Energy — Healed Healers

Especially those NDErs who have merged with the Light, find themselves the victims of an exciting and alien energy.

> You won't believe this, but I get electrical sparks in my hands that drive me crazy...it's funny. This energy goes around and around: it's like I'll feel a buildup and my hands will start to tingle: they'll actually hurt. [Do they feel hot?] Hot? You can feel the heat pouring out of them! It's like they are on fire. [Did anything like this occur to you before your incident?] Never. Never...It's like an electrical shock going right through you. But powerfully, really powerfully.

Researchers like Ring and Grey have called this energy Kundalini, the subtle spiritual energy raised up the spine through the practice of Yoga. Though it is possible that Kundalini is aroused during or after the NDE, it appears more likely that the energy absorbed in the NDE is celestial or Holy Spirit energy.

By whatever name, the new energy can be problematic as well as creative. During an ecstatic, energetic "high," individuals are inspired and active, but may be unable to sleep.

The sudden acquisition of spiritual energy can be debilitating in other ways as well, and a knowledgeable spiritual teacher may be needed. However, the energy also heals, and results in the NDErs ability to heal others.

One NDEr was healed, in the NDE, by the light of Christ:

> Suddenly I seemed to be right in front of the being standing there. He was standing with the light behind him and I had the dark behind me, so I was actually facing the light. I came up to within what seemed like about a foot away from his face...I looked at this being and there was just enough light on his face for me to tell that it was what I took to be an elder person. I could see the wrinkles around his eyes, he had a long straight face, no beard, but piercing eyes and white hair. I was not aware if he had on a robe or what he was wearing, only that he was looking right through me. He — I was trying to make up my mind who he was: I know it was Christ...As he stood looking at me he said the following: "That's enough, it's dead, it's gone." I don't remember how I got back to the hospital room or into my body...But I do know what he meant when he said, "It's dead." To me it meant that the germ was dead. It's gone, I no longer have leukemia.

A British gentleman, after several incidents of self healing also discovered he could heal others. A self-healing occurred during wine-making:

> I...was pouring three gallons of boiling water on to the mush, when a couple of friends called. Whilst talking and carrying on with the job, I

put my hands and arms into the water and began stirring. One of my friends shouted at me, and I, suddenly aware of what I had done, pulled my hands out of the water, and was amazed to find that there was no pain, scalding or blister.

His first healing of another happened:

> One evening [as] I was talking to a friend and his wife, who had been deaf in one ear since childhood, when he suddenly asked me to put my hands on his wife's faulty ear. In a minute or two, taking my hands away, she said, "I can hear."

Grace has returned from a vegetative state through the strength given to her by her "Lord." Dianne had lupus and little energy prior to her NDE. She now has so much energy she is searching for an outlet in the helping professions. Dianne can control her lupus by mentally applying Light to the affected areas, and heals others through touch and prayer. Though the public is beginning to appreciate "wholistic" health, and the medical profession is more open to alterntive treatment, gifts like Dianne's remain under-utilized.

The NDE precipitates psychological health as well as physical healing. Barbara Harris' account of her psychological healing is similar to other NDErs who are healed of a life-time of accumulated hurts and defenses.

> At that point, I left. . . it's not clear to me which happened when, but I went back into the tunnel and I really wanted to die. . . And I saw myself in bed, crying, the way I had just left myself, only I was a little child. And my mother was there and my father was there . . . This was such an intense experience, it was like I was there again. Everything was clearly the way it was when I was that small child. I was that child again. If there were any aromas, I was picking up aromas. I was picking up all the physical sensa-tions of my mother hitting me again, yet at the same time, besides my feel-ings, I understood her feelings and I understood my father in the hallway. . .
> I was saying "no wonder. No wonder you are the way you are," you know? I look at my kids now and I think if I'd done that to them every night how would they feel? You know, I could see it from all angles now as an adult but at the same time I was experiencing it at maybe the age of four or five. And it was the kind of a thing that I knew where my dad was coming from. I knew all the connections. That was it. I could feel our connectedness in this scene.
> And then it was like I moved through, on to where I am now . . . I don't want to give the idea that this was linear, because it wasn't linear. It was almost like that might have been the focal point and then things would branch out in every direction and I was getting different connections with different people. It was like I was understanding how insecure I was and how

inferior I felt because nobody had put their arms around me and given me a sense of value. Now this was my adult, my real adult observer. Then I was able to see my whole life unwinding from that perspective of this poor neurotic little girl who was, you know, not really coming from the same place all the other little kids were coming from. I was a very, very lonely child. I was watching this whole childhood unfold and realizing that my head was in the wrong place and I was able to refocus so that I had a better understanding of all the rejection I had felt. All that rejection was in my own head. It wasn't everybody else rejecting me. Everyone else was just coming from their own problems and hangups. All of that stuff had been layered on me because my vision of what was going on was really screwed up. [So it was like a corrective review of your life?] Yeah. It was like the most healing therapy there could be. . . Years and years of intense psychoanalysis or the most intense type of external therapy could not have brought me through what I was experiencing rapidly. I was forgiving myself for not always being good. I was forgiving myself for being neurotic as I had been. [And I felt] a great deal of forgiveness and compassion for people that I thought were being mean to me. There was just a great deal of understanding that we had formed a bad pattern because of defensiveness in my entire life and I had put them into the mold they were in of treating me, to the point where I actualized that treatment. And I could understand their beauties and qualities. And it was like all the slates were being wiped clean. . . It was the kind of thing where I just wasn't the victim anymore; we had all been victims . . . the structure was becoming stronger and stronger of us victimizing each other and it seemed like I was able to just very objectively observe it . . . we were just establishing more and more walls. And I was able to just understand everything that was going on.

[Did you actually see these scenes like images, or were you just aware of this?] OK. This is very, very hard to explain . . . What I was really sensing was that I had layers and layers and layers of this stuff. Like the domino effect, the sudden realization from the beginning was just going through and everything was just shifting. Like each electron was jumping into another orbit. It was like a healing. It was going right through me. And I was sensing this entire evolvement of my lifetime through my feelings and, wherever I wanted to, I could sort of zoom in on different huge events in my life maybe I felt were good or bad — but there was no good or bad, just me re-experiencing stuff. . .

The whole overall effect was that I had relived my life with a much healthier attitude that had healed me. And by the time I got to the end I had the first sense of wanting to live, of wanting to turn around and struggle again in that bed.

On the whole, then, the NDE is physically and psychologically healing. The process of healing has, however, just begun. Time and hard work are required to consolidate the new sense of self, as Barb has pointed out, and to understand and integrate the NDE.

Religious Revelation and Spiritual Renewal

The NDE precipitates spiritual, as well as physical and emotional changes. Though a Roman Catholic before her NDE, Dianne now practices Yoga. Howard is studying theology in seminary. His universal religious perspective appears in conflict with the orthodox Christian position on the uniqueness of Christ. Tom Sawyer, an atheist before his experience, now knows there is a God, like one of Ring's respondents:

> Essentially, at the same time of my accident, I was a ranting, raving atheist. There was no God...He was a figment of man's imagination...(now) I know that there's a God...Everything that exists has the essence of God within it.
>
> Now I think of God as a tremendous source of energy, like the nucleus of something enormous, and that we are all just separate atoms from this nucleus. I think God is in everyone of us. We are God.

The NDE is a profoundly spiritual experience. It is an immediate and personal experience that influences attitudes toward religion (or the externals of worship) and spirituality (or the inner dimension). While each NDE is unique, there is a common thread throughout, illustrated by Dianne, Howard and Tom. According to Ken Ring, NDErs return with a universal, pluralistic and spiritual religious perspective; and they are convinced that God, or at least an aspect of divinity, is real, as is the Afterlife. Life does not end with death.

> I know there is life after death. Nobody can shake my belief. I have no doubt — it's peaceful and nothing to be feared. I don't know what's beyond what I experienced, but it's plenty for me....I only know that death is not to be feared, only dying.
>
> I have a message to others living an ordinary earth life to tell them. There is more. Our identity will continue to be — in a greater way. Friends will not be lost to you. You will know a beauty and peace and love [and] that the loving light that encompasses and fills you is God.

A universal attitude toward who qualifies for heaven proceeds from the discovery of the oneness of all religions like the NDEr who says:

> All religions started from the same truth, and there is little variation between the major belief of each. What a great tool this will be to at last begin to unify mankind under one God, one truth and spiritual belief.

" 'The Lord is One.' That is what all my searching after the near-death experience has brought me to. That we are all one. All of us. This prayer [the 'Shema Y'Israel'] affirms the unity of our oneness with God." Barbara

Harris' universal attitude expressed in this affirmation of the unity of all traditions does not prevent a pluralistic approach. She appreciates the beauty in each religion.

> At rituals like Rosh Hashanah, before I always used to stand back as an observer and sometimes it replused me. After the near-death experience, I became more open-minded and observed and respected it. And I really got into the beauty of the ritual. The Hebrew chanting just absolutely took me away. The rabbi raising the shofar, which is a ram's horn that they blow to signify the New Year — the beauty of knowing that all over the world, in every synagogue, the ram's horn is being blown to signify the New Year. It's just — I have goose pimples just telling you this . . . What ever type of organized religion I see now, I really enjoy. I really admire Catholicism — the color, the ritual . . .

Spiritual renewal accomplished in the NDE continues through a relationship with the Lord, Presence, Voice, Light or spiritual being encountered in heaven. NDErs often continue to have direct contact with the divine dimension, and like the woman below, stress this relationship more than the externals of church worship:

> Since then [the near-death experience] I can't say that I've gone to Church any more, but I feel I'm a more religious person. I find myself praying, not in a structured kind of way, but just praying more than I ever did when I went to Church. I mean, you went to Church because it's kind of the thing to do, but now I find that I pray just because it comes out of me . . .

Mystics are united in a common experience, like the NDEr. They are more like each other than the ordinary worshipper in any of the world's religious traditions. They, too, tend to be experiential, spiritual, universal and pluralistic. By virtue of the spiritual and religious changes, as well as the other aftereffects, the NDEr has entered the ancient community of mystics.

Many NDErs turn to Eastern traditions, which emphasize the meditative spiritual element, in order to continue spiritual growth. Others may wish to retain membership in a Western worshipping community and look for spiritual guidance there. Unlike Grace, whose experience was specifically Christian, and whose pastor was receptive, remaining or becoming Christian may prove difficult. Protestants on the whole prefer a secular, social Christianity. Roman Catholics appear to reserve true mysticism for the monasteries. It may be difficult, if not impossible, to find Christian spiritual direction and teaching that affirms the reality of otherworldly experience, at least in the established churches.

Christians who remain in their congregations and share their experiences and attitudes may find themselves persecuted for their beliefs. Religious persecution is, however, less life-threatening than it used to be. The largest threat to NDErs' life and health is persecution by family, friends, and clinical specialists, who think the NDErs are mad.

The label of "crazy" has caused some NDErs to be institutionalized, silenced others with subsequent clinical depression, alienated NDErs from their families, who may label them insane, resulted in the clinical use of drugs, which is contra-indicated in cases of spiritual crisis, and been a factor in a child custody case:

> After Elaine Winner was revived in Mercy Hospital in Chicago, she faced three years of torment and mental anguish. A skeptical medical community and public that was largely ignorant of the phenomenon made it very difficult for her to explain what she had experienced.
>
> "I felt totally alone," recalled Winner. "I began wondering about my sanity. There are so many experiencers out there who need to be reached," she said. "They need to be told they are not crazy, that they are not alone and that they should not be afraid of being made fun of."
>
> But Winner paid a dear price to openly reveal her life-changing experience; her husband, Charles, divorced her and alienated their two daughters, Cheryl, 18, and Rose, 14. The two girls live with Charles in Florence, Kentucky, though Cheryl has recently moved temporarily into her mother's house in Indiana.
>
> "My father told me she was crazy," said Cheryl. "It scared him when she talked about seeing the dead." Winner, now remarried, recently read her hospital medical files and found out Charles had succeeded in gaining custody of the girls by persuading the court that she was mentally unstable.

Mystical giants of western Christendom suffered similar persecution. We in the West have a penchant for persecution of mystics and posthumous canonization. Perhaps we can learn from the past in order to minimize the pain and suffering of the mystics in our midst. If we continue to cut them to fit the procrustean beds of psychiatric diagnoses or secular materialistic consciousness, they will populate our psychiatric institutions instead of pulpits, lecture platforms and the helping professions.

Chapter 6

Mysticism

I thought I was being carried up to Heaven: the first persons I saw there were my mother and father, and such great things happened in so short a time...I wish I could give a description of at least the smallest part of what I learned, but when I try to discover a way of doing so, I find it impossible, for while the light we see here and that other light are both light, there is no comparison between the two and the brightness of the sun seems quite dull if compared with the other. [Afterwards] I was...left with very little fear of death, of which previously I had been very much afraid.

That is no NDEr speaking, but the great Christian mystic St. Theresa of Avila decribing what happened to her during the raptures which accompany contemplative prayer or meditation.

The resemblance between Theresa's experience and the NDErs we have met is remarkable, but are they the same? In what ways is the NDEr like the mystic and what distinguish the two? Near-death researchers have called the NDE an experience of mystical illumination and a spontaneous spiritual experience, but what do they mean?

As I pondered these questions, I was aware that while near-death research had introduced the subjects of mysticism and spirituality, no one had pursued them either by asking such questions or seeking answers from spiritual disciplines. Here I intend to extend the near-death discussion into the realm of the spiritual and mystical in a simple way. I compare the life-long mystical experiences of two Christian mystics, St. Theresa of Avila and St. John of the Cross, to the NDE and its aftereffects. In doing so, I discover the relationship between these mystics and most NDErs to be more remarkable than we supposed. Many NDErs have had a profound mystical experience. I also began to suspect that mysticism was, roughly, the Christian equivalent of spirituality in other traditions, and I use the terms interchangeably.

In the comparison of experience to experience, the rough outline of the mystical-spiritual dimension of the NDE appears. We can now recognize some NDEs as mystical experience, and the NDEr as some kind of mystic. The details of the picture begin to emerge, however, when the NDE is compared to models of mystical/spiritual growth. On closer inspection, not all NDEs are spiritually similar, and most NDErs have not attained the heights of spiritual consciousness.

It is important to know these two things: that many NDErs have had a mystical experience, but they are not yet perfected mystics or even saints. The awareness of the mystical element of the NDE is needed by everyone — NDErs, family, friends, counselors, so that they can be treated with compassionate understanding. It is also important for everyone to know that they are not yet perfected saints in order to fight inflation and prevent the pedestal effect.

The NDEr may desire to begin or continue a spiritual practice, preferably on one of the spiritual paths attached to the world's religions, to convert the spiritual treasure discovered during the NDE into a permanent asset. These paths are available for the NDEr to continue spiritual growth and learn techniques for reentry, and also for those who hope to have a near-death like experience. There, through thousands of years, the understanding of the dimension of spirit has been developed, and teachers have been trained and legitimized to lead the disciple into the other world and back to earth again. Within the spiritual paths exist the techniques to accomplish transcendence, the intellectual comprehension that accompanies that experience, and the tools for effective reentry. The spiritual paths of the world's religions should be the authority on spiritual/mystical experience. That is their field.

Many NDErs have had their experiences recognized by legitimate spiritual teachers. This should, I believe, be the "mark" of a mystical experience. It takes one to know one. What the spiritual teacher knows is that many NDErs have transcended the realm of this world and ordinary consciousness. They have become, if only for a moment, citizens of heaven. They have had a taste of the other, after life. Now they need to get to know the spiritual world as intimately as this one. They need more training. One mystical experience does not make a mystic. A mystic intentionally practices a spiritual discipline toward achievement of the goals established by his or her tradition. The practice of mysticism is within the capacity of everyone, but not all are called. The few that choose, or are chosen, risk their lives to lead us "home."

The NDE, then, is one of a broader group of experiences called mystical or spiritual. Death offers an opportunity for mystical experience, as does childbirth, personal crisis, attending the death of another, or simply spontaneously. The NDE has achieved public visibility, credibility and clarity for mystical experience in general. The twelve million NDErs represent a larger, unknown, and for the most part silent, minority: the masses of Americans who have had transcendent experiences.

To say one has had an NDE means something specific. To say one has had a mystical experience can mean anything or nothing. I believe that the introduction of the NDE into the larger category of mystical experience can serve to clarify the meaning of "mystical" to the public, the individual mystic, and the seeker. If one has had an experience similar to an NDE, with attendant light, love, information and especially transformation, then one has had a mystical experience. The secular materialist and the spiritual seeker both need to be aware that there are spiritual realities and those trained and capable of making that distinction. As the saints and sages set standards against which to judge the NDE, so, too, can the NDE set standards for the spiritual seeker who is unclear about spiritual realities or reluctant to leave the realm of psychic phenomena.

Though the inclusion of the NDE in the larger group of mystical experiences makes the issue of "death" a moot point (except for those NDErs who discover that fact has been eliminated from their hospital records), death has always been a factor on the spiritual path, or mystic way. A great Sufi teacher has called mysticism "learning to die before you die." For the Christian mystics Theresa and John, mysticism was both the reason for life, and a preparation for death. On the spiritual path, the soul becomes pure enough to blend into the light, and during ecstasy the soul glimpses the afterlife, according to Theresa.

> I think . . . that this experience has been of great help to me in teaching me where our true home is and in showing me that on earth we are but pilgrims; it is a great thing to see what is waiting us there and to know where we are going to live. For if a person has to go and settle in another country, it is a great help to him in bearing the trials of the journey if he has found out that it is a country where he will be able to live in complete comfort.

Not only death, but the NDE has also been intimately connected with Christian mysticism. Many of the great mystics began their path with one. Scholar Elizabeth Petroff tells us that:

> A surprising number of biographies and autobiographies tell of an apparent dying, often when a teenager, of being taken for dead and perhaps even put in a coffin but then miraculously coming back to life, often with an explicit visionary message for the world. This happened to Christina Mirabilis, Catherine of Siena, Magdalena Beuthler, St. Theresa of Avila, and Julian of Norwich.

And Zalesky has pointed to the historic development of mysticism from the NDE.

> The near-death medieval narratives . . . correspond to what historian Peter Dinzelbacher calls the first phase of medieval Christian vision literature (lasting until the mid-thirteenth century) in which the visionary travels out of his or her body to visit heaven, hell and purgatory, and returns to life transformed.

Though united in a common intimacy with death, NDErs and mystics differ, however, in intention, preparation, understanding and techniques and communities for reintegration. On the spiritual path, growth is slow. Each experience is accompanied by an integration of the emotional, intellectual, physical components of the individual. Unlike the mystic, the NDEr is suddenly jettisoned unprepared into another world and the higher reaches of spiritual consciousness. Often the NDEr must make up emotional and intellectual deficiencies by entering school, counseling, a new career, or a spiritual path.

Unlike the mystic, NDErs return to an alien community rather than a monastery. They return to a culture dominated by secular materialism, with little understanding of and less interest in mysticism. They, themselves, may misunderstand their own experience. The difficult task of reentering life and recovery from death is compounded by the often negative feed-back provided the NDEr by his-her own community. The conflicts and tensions that result may create pathology where previously only a penchant for mysticism existed.

Comparison of the NDE and Aftereffects with the
Mysticism of St. Theresa of Avila and
St. John of the Cross

The sixteenth century Spanish world of St. Theresa of Avila and St. John of the Cross was equally dangerous in a different way. Fear of the Inquisition silenced many mystics. St. John of the Cross did not speak openly about his mystical experiences, but disguised them in the metaphoric nuances of poetry. Theresa, however, did write of her mystical experience in *The Autobiography of Theresa of Jesus*. Because of her courage we have a legacy of personal mystical experience to compare to the modern near-death accounts. Any NDEr unfamiliar with Theresa's writings will be surprised, I believe, to discover that from beginning to end of her mystical career, Theresa appeared to experience the same events as an NDE.

Theresa's may have been a different style of mysticism from the Christian norm, but she has been accorded a high status by the Church. She was the spiritual companion and friend of the mystical doctor of the Church, St. John of the Cross. They understood, aided and abetted one another in their earthly careers, as well as spiritual journeys. Theresa tells us, in her own words, about her ecstatic out-of-body spiritual experiences.

> Turning now to this sudden transport of the spirit it may be said . . . that the soul really seems to have left the body; on the other hand it is clear that the person is not dead . . . He feels as if he had been in another world, very different from this in which we live, and has been shown a fresh light

there, so much unlike any to be found in this life long, it would have been impossible for him to obtain any idea of them. In a single instant he is taught so many things all at once, that, if he were to labor for years on end in trying to fit them all into his imagination and thought, he could not succeed with a thousandth part of them. This . . . is seen with the eyes of the soul very much more clearly than we can see things with the eyes of the body; and some of the revelations are communicated to it [the soul] without words.

During rapture, Theresa obtains all knowledge instantaneously and telepathically like the NDEr. She also has a "life review," for in rapture, "Its past life comes up before it and all the truth of God's great mercy is revealed."

Theresa loses all fear of death during a rapturous flight to heaven. NDErs also lose fear of death, as one declares.

If that is what death is like, then I'm not afraid to go . . . If that's anyway like the hereafter is, then I'm not afraid to go at all. I have absolutely no fear at all . . . I'm not afraid of dying. I'm really not afraid and I used to be scared to death.

The similarity of Theresa's mystical experience to the NDE doesn't end with a heavenly journey. Having tasted death, both are capable of seeing the souls of the dying. Among many such instances, Theresa recounts:

Another friar of our Order — a very good friar — was extremely ill; and while I was at Mass I became recollected and saw that he was dead and was ascending into Heaven without passing through purgatory. He had died, as I afterward hear, at the very hour at which I saw him.

Ring discovered during his research that:

Seeing apparitions of dead persons is by no means as rare as many people think . . . and there are several such cases from my own files. Often these forms seem to coincide with the time of their death. A suggestive example of this was furnished by one of my correspondents who had her near-death experience in 1953. She writes: "Five years ago, my brother, age fifty-two, passed away. At 4:00 A.M. that day, I was awakened by a soft, luminous light at the foot of my bed. It slowly ascended upward and disappeared. Half an hour later, I was notified of his passing, exactly at 4:00 A.M. While the light was present, I felt extremely tranquil and didn't move."

Theresa's rapturous flights, during which it feels as if the soul has left the cold and almost lifeless body behind, are her entrance into heaven where see sees the light, obtains all knowledge, visits dead relatives, has a life-review and loses fear of death, just as the typical NDEr. Despite the pain accompanying rapture, Theresa, too, often returned healed of any illness and stronger and more energetic than before. Others were not so fortunate. "There are people of so frail a constitution that one experience of the Prayer of Quiet has killed them."

This Prayer of Quiet (a high degree of contemplative prayer) is marked for Theresa by love and bliss and marred by the mistaken madness of poetic and confused utterance. "I used often to commit follies because of this love and to be inebriated," she says, like Howard who hugged everyone when he returned. Theresa also composed poetry at this stage and was unable to reason, "Many words are spoken during this state, in praise of God, but unless the Lord Himself puts order into them, they have no orderly form." At this stage Theresa exhibits the metaphoric and confused speech of the mystic that is often thought to be psychotic psychobabble. She, too, was called mad and tells her superior, "I beseech your Reverance, let us all be mad for the Love of Him who was called mad for our sakes."

The Prayer of Quiet brings with it a degree of detachment from the world which is deepened during rapture, a desire for solitude, and a yearning to die to be with God. "What," however, Theresa wonders, "will the soul experience when it regains its senses and goes back to live in the world and has to return to the world's preoccupations and formalities?" She will discover the same changes as the NDEr, which she considers gifts and virtues; and she will suffer similar persecutions.

Mystical Virtues and Near-Death Values

During the beginning or purgatorial stage of the mystic way, effort is required to practice the virtues of detachment from wealth, status and personal relationship. Rapture brings achievement when, according to Theresa:

> The Lord helps and transforms a soul, so that it seems no longer to be itself, or even its own likeness . . . It is no longer bound by ties of relationship, friendship or property. Previously all its acts of will and resolutions and desires were powerless to loosen these and seemed only to bind them the more . . .

The NDEr also no longer cares for wealth or status.

> ". . . Before I was living for material things . . . Before I was conscious of only me, what I had, what I wanted . . . I have gradually sloughed off the desires to have and to hold earthly possessions, material possessions to any great degree . . ."

Competitive status seeking so prevalent in our culture is perceived by another NDEr as false.

> Now...I'm starting to see that God didn't want me as a professional psychologist, dragging in the big bucks, getting all involved with the big words and labels for other people's conditions, and me getting all puffed up with my importance. He has made me a candle, lighting the place where I am.

Apparently the frantic search for wealth and material status which characterizes our culture has nothing to do with what the NDEr learns is the meaning of life, which is "...love. Fulfilling yourself with that love — by giving."

The NDE expands the capacity to feel and express other emotions, as well as love. When remembering the light, NDErs often weep copious tears. Theresa, too, shed tears of joy during her raptures. They were for her a validation that the experience was real. Theresa was not alone. Petroff tells us that:

> In the middle ages, women mystics often wept uncontrollably: among them Marie d'Oignies, Angela of Oligno and Margery Kempe... For Angela of Foligno and Margery Kempe, tears were accompanied by loud sobbing resulting in embarrassment for them and their supporters.

The weeping of the mystics was called "the gift of tears." The supernatural visions and voices which accompany the mystic life were also considered gifts.

Visions and Voices

Theresa heard the Voice of her Lord during her entire life. At times He was her only companion and counsel. Theresa believed these supernatural experiences to be divine favors, and offers advice for distinguishing between the Voice of God and the works of the devil. If the experience is powerful, memorable and has a good effect upon the soul, it can be said to come from God. NDERs never forget their experience, even if they try. The most wonderful event of their lives leaves them more compassionate, energetic and eager to serve God and humanity in some helping capacity. The practice of humility and divine thanksgiving saved Theresa from the dangers and abuses of these divine gifts.

On the other hand, St. John of the Cross is aware of the dangers inherent in these supernatural gifts, and warns the spiritual aspirant to become empty of all mental content, both natural and supernatural, in favor of a "vague, dark and general knowledge" which is the goal of contemplation and the earthly equivalent of the clear light of the other world. NDErs, too, often forget the details of the "big secret" while retaining the sense of what they learned during the NDE.

St. John of the Cross, however, affirms that supernatural events do occur in the life of the spiritual aspirant. "Spiritual persons can, and usually do, perceive visions of images and persons from the other life; of saints, of the good and bad angels and of unusual lights and splendors. Through hearing they apprehend certain extraordinary words..." Supernatural images are given to lead creatures from sense, to supernatural sense and then to pure spirit which is beyond all form. John's way of "nada" or nothing includes emptying of all human content, of personal intellect memory and will, as well as voiding the supernatural visions and voices which follow a spiritual awakening. NDErs, too, often lose pre-NDE memory, the ability to do discursive thinking, and relinquish their personal will to God.

Though John does not discuss his experiences, in *The Ascent of Mt. Carmel* he provides instructions to those who pass through the stage of supernatural visions in their ascent to the God who is beyond all form. In *The Ascent* he discusses all of the supernatural visions and voices the aspirant is likely to encounter, including "revelations" which are "the intellectual understanding of truths about God, or...a vision of present, past or future events which bear resemblance to the spirit of prophecy."

Tom Sawyer, as well as other NDErs, has this clairvoyant and prophetic ability. Tom has told me that he views all events now in 3-D. He can see all the causes that have led to an event and perceive eventual outcomes. Tom can also intuitively read a person's heart. John of the Cross "affirms that those who have reached perfection or are already close to it usually possess light and knowledge about events happening in their presence or absence...and can perceive the talents of men and what lies in their hearts." These supernatural talents are signs, then, of spiritual growth, and are only to be avoided because they detain the spiritual aspirant on his or her journey to the God who is beyond all images, or serve as occasions for spiritual inflation.

Knowledge of this kind is a side-effect of spiritual growth, and according to John, should not be sought for its own sake. "These kinds of knowledge come" he says, "to the soul passively, and thereby exclude any active endeavor of the soul." John, however, utilizes these gifts when appropriate, but suggests caution in case the knowledge is wrong. John also believes that the word of God is never to be taken literally. One must look for the hidden significance. Together, Theresa and John are excellent guides for the discrimination and utilization of spiritual gifts. They affirm the reality of supernatural events, but each in his or her own way urges caution concerning the exercise of psychic and spiritual gifts which accompany all genuine mystical experience.

The task of supernatural hearing or seeing strains the psyche. Communicating mystical experience to those who have not had one is equally difficult.

Theresa complains of the same essential "ineffability" which plagues NDErs' attempts to explain a spiritual experience in earthly language. "However clearly I may wish to describe these matters which concern prayer," she says, "they will be very obscure to anyone who has not experience of it...Anyone who has attained to raptures will, I know, understand it well. If he has not experienced it, it will seem ridiculous."

The mystic, like the NDEr, must resort to a language derived from and meant for an earthly existence, in order to explain the spiritual world and other-worldly experience. Theresa and John often resort to metaphor, which is the only way to suggest similarity without sameness. As listeners, we are likely to reduce spiritual experience to ordinary events in the world. We may feel they are only metaphors, which do not refer to a real, though extraordinary experience. Or we think they are ridiculous.

"Anticipation of ridicule or doubts about their sanity," Zalesky says, "prevent the NDEr from speaking about their experience." Silence, however, presents as great a risk as speaking. NDErs who remain silent never heal. Talking about the experience may be part of their personal healing and the healing of the culture, but to speak requires courage. Women mystics suffered from the same conflict between speech and silence, according to Petroff.

> Many women mystics speak of a period of illness that precedes their decisions to write down their experiences. They are fearful about what they expect to be a negative response to their writing, yet inwardly compelled to speak publicly of what they have experienced. The resolution to their dilemma comes only when a divine voice tells them they must write. Once they begin, they find that it is a healing process and that they gain strength from articulating what they know about the spiritual life.

Pain and Persecution

NDErs who gather the courage to speak of their experiences meet with envy, fear, ridicule and skepticism, as did St. Theresa when people learned of her raptures and supernatural favors.

> When this [her raptures] became known, people began to have a good opinion of one whose wickedness all were not fully aware...Then suddenly began evil-speaking and persecution...They said that I wanted to become a saint and that I was inventing new-fangled practices.

Apparently Theresa, like the NDEr, suffered from the "pedestal effect:" first undeservedly elevated and then persecuted. A number of NDErs that I know complain that their families alternatively view them as saints or insane.

Neither is true. NDErs, like Theresa in the early stages of her mystical career, are not yet perfected saints. Nor are they mad, as society called St. Theresa of Avila, St. Francis of Assisi and now the NDEr.

Theresa's most serious persecution, however, came from those who believed she was possessed by the devil, as some fundamentalist Christians accuse NDErs. Theresa was forbidden to pray or to be alone or go to communion. This went on for two years, until she found someone who had shared her experience and knew it was of value. "But just then," she complained, "I needed someone who had gone through it all for such a person alone could understand me and interpret my experience."

Elaine Winner also complains of the loneliness that followed her NDE.

> I felt totally alone. I began wondering about my sanity . . . I didn't know what to do, who to turn to . . . I was frustrated and I begged God to let me die again — I wanted the pleasantness. There are so many experiencers out there who need to be reached, she said. The need to be told they are not crazy, that they are not alone and that they should not be afraid of being made fun of.

Elaine had entered the "dark night of the soul," like Theresa who, alienated from the world and abandoned by God, felt "Crucified between heaven and earth."

By virtue of these shared experiences and changes, the NDEr has often unwittingly entered the ancient and honorable community of mystics. They share with the "communion of saints" a common world view that differs from our ordinary one. However, they have not yet become perfected mystics or saints. To retain the spiritual treasure and continue growth toward higher mystical states, NDErs might seek a competent guide or spiritual director. Unfortunately, there is always a dearth of both experienced and learned Christian spiritual directors to guide the more advanced souls. Poor spiritual direction was a trial to both Theresa and John, who considered it an aspect of the dark night. Theresa had "come across souls so constrained and afflicted by the inexperience of their director that I have felt really sorry for them." Our time is little different. The contemporary Carmellite, Father McNamara, finds "qualified . . . spiritual directors rare these days, in the Dark Night of the Church." It is my hope that the reality of the NDE will modify the present tendency of Christian spiritual directors to reduce mysticism to ordinary reality, and revitalize the supernatural ecstasy of St. John and St. Theresa.

Stages of Christian Mysticism

The stages of the Christian mystic way are: (1) Purgation-Beginner, (2) Illumination-Proficient, and (3) Union-Perfect. At the stage of beginner, the spiritual pupil does all the work, and God does very little. Discipline is required to remain in prayer or meditation, and to detach from the things of this world. In the later stages, according to Theresa, God begins to do the work through the gift of ecstatic raptures. The act of purgation, or cleansing the soul of negativity, however, continues throughout the spiritual journey.

The second stage of the mystic way, illumination, is achieved through a vision of a real, unearthly light, according to mystical scholar Evelyn Underhill.

> What is the nature of this mysterious illumination? Apart from the message it transmits, what is the form which it most usually assumes in the consciousness of self? The illuminatives, one and all, seem to assure us that its apparently symbolic name is a realistic one; that it appears to them as a kind of radiance, a flooding of the personality with new light... "Light rare, untellable!" said Whitman. "The flowing light of the Godhead," said Mechtild of Magdeburg, trying to describe what it was that made the difference between her universe and that of normal men. "Lux vivens dicit," said Hildegard of her revelations, which she described as appearing in a special light, more brilliant than the brightness around the sun. It is an "infused brightness," says St. Theresa, "a light which knows no night; but rather as it is always light, nothing ever disturbs it."

The NDEr who has seen this light can vouch for its reality. They have had an experience of mystical illumination. Therefore, they have left the rank of beginner, and entered the mystic way. They have crossed the threshold between natural and supernatural vision, between ordinary and superordinary consciousness, and may be called proficient.

The final goal of Christian mysticism is, however, God union. St. John of the Cross describes this as a union of the soul with the Trinity of Love, Power and Wisdom of which Love is the first cause and Light is the principal. NDErs who encounter the Light experience this totality of Love, Power and Wisdom, like one anonymous narrator:

> It was a dynamic light, not like a spotlight. It was an incredible energy — a light you wouldn't believe. I almost floated in it. It was feeding my consciousness feelings of unconditional love, complete safety, and complete, total perfection...It just dived into you. My consciousness was going out and getting larger and taking in more; I expanded and more and more came in. It was such rapture, such bliss. And then, and then, a piece of knowledge came in, it was that I was immortal... Later when I was saying the Lord's Prayer, and I got to that part that says "thine is the kingdom, and the power and the glory," I thought that nothing could describe this experience any better. It was pure power and glory...it was in, around and through everything. It is what halos are made of. It is God made visible.

As NDErs are transformed when united with the Light, so are mystics. According to John, union with the Light transforms or "divinizes" the soul, for "He created her in his image and likeness that she might attain such resemblance." In divinization:

> God makes the soul die to all that He is not, so that. . . He may clothe it anew. . . This renovation is an illumination of the human intellect with supernatural light so that it becomes divine, united with the divine: an informing of the will with love of God so that it is no longer less than divine and loves in no other way than divinely. . . And this soul will be a soul of heaven, heavenly and more divine than human.

Entering or merging with the Light during an NDE results in a spiritual transformation of the soul which, however, may be only temporary and therefore imperfect. Even those NDErs who have momentarily achieved the heights of mystical consciousness need to continue their spiritual work upon return, to turn that glimpse into permanent attainment.

Christian mysticism may emphasize the Light, but a number of respected mystics speak of the Darkness of God beyond the light, or a paradoxical union of light and darkness at the highest levels of mystical awareness. Dionysius the Aereopagite speaks of a self-loss "wherein we pass beyond the topmost altitudes of the ascent, and leave behind all divine illuminations and voices and heavenly utterances; and plunge into the darkness where truly dwells, as scripture saith, that one which is beyond all things."

The contemporary Christian mystic Bernadette Roberts underwent an experience of loss of self into a condition which she describes as "no-self." Prior to that final loss of self, she experienced some of the same paranormal phenomena as the NDEr or the mystic Theresa.

> Matters stood this way for twenty years [the interior flame of union was stable] when suddenly, in this phase, there was a movement in the center, deep inexplicable rumblings which gave me the idea of an impending explosion. When the thermostat was turned up, there came with it an energy never encountered before, a problematic energy in that it gave rise to a rash of extra-ordinary experiences, fore knowledge, knowledge of others, and even the possibility of healing. Whatever the true nature of these energies, it was obvious they wanted to reach outside and find expression. I felt about to be used as a medium for these powers, and what this meant, I had no idea.

Roberts chose to ignore these as alien to her experience and says that "from the start, I can compare this difficult regime to sitting on a volcano or riding a bronco." The sudden explosion of alien energy and extraordinary experiences served as a prelude, for Roberts, to a higher state of mystical consciousness.

The mystical way therefore proceeds in stages that resemble the phases of the NDE. First, the NDEr exits the body, but remains in an earthly environment. During this stage certain paranormal phenomena occur. Though the events and aftereffects may be called psychic, they are not yet truly mystical. Travel through a dark tunnel toward a bright light represents the transition from this world to the next. The NDEr then either enters heaven, or encounters the Light before return to life. The vision of heavenly light constitutes an experience of Christian illumination, while encountering, entering or merging with the Light fulfills the requirements of Christian union, however transient. Hence, at each phase of the NDE, a higher stage of mystical consciousness is achieved. That this is true is further suggested by the fact that fewer people reach the deeper stages of the NDE, as few mystics attain the heights of mystical perfection.

In general, according to my own informal observation, those who abort at the OBE phase may return as psychics, but not mystics. Those who enter heaven may encounter specific spiritual beings, usually from their own tradition, and return as converts to a specific religious tradition. Entrance into the Light or Darkness of God usually results in a more universal spirituality, in which the new mystic feels at home in all the spiritual traditions of the world. This difference in depth of NDE, as measured by the phase at which the experience ends, may therefore account for the differences in religious and spiritual responses that occur together with a more universal spirituality.

Universal Stages of Transpersonal Consciousness

The relationship between near-death phases and mystical stages is further strengthened by examining a universal model of mystical consciousness developed by transpersonal psychologist Ken Wilber. Using a template of the world's spiritual traditions, Wilber discovered a series of stages of consciousness which transcend our ordinary rational ego. In *Spiritual Choices*, Wilber has reduced an array of post-rational stages to three: The first stage or The Psychic, during which psychic phenomena may occur, though generally characterized by a thought process he calls vision-logic, in which everything is seen as connected to everything else. The second stage, or Subtle, is the stage of visions of diety and of illuminations. Wilber's final stage, the Causal, is the stage beyond images: the Void, Formlessness, the Ground of Being. This is the highest state of mystical consciousness, the Darkness of God beyond images, achieved by Roberts and Wren-Lewis as well as Meister Eckart, Dionysius, presumably St. John of the Cross and others. According to this scheme, the Light is probably a prelude to experiencing God as divine Darkness. (See Table 2 for a comparison of near-death phases, stages of Christian mysticism and transpersonal consciousness.)

Wilber, then, speaks of states or stages of consciousness while NDErs and mystics often talk of going to heaven. The great mystical scholar Evelyn Underhill believes that they are the same. As she says:

> Just as the normal consciousness stands over against the unconscious, which, with its buried impulses and its primitive and infantile cravings, represents a cruder reaction of the organism to the external world; so does the development of mystical life stand over against normal consciousness, with its preoccupations and its web of illusions . . . Reviewing the firsthand declarations of the mystics, we invariably notice one prominent feature; the frequency with which they break up their experience into three phases. Sometimes they regard these objectively and speak of three worlds or three aspects of God of which they become successively aware [this world, the Eternal World, and the Eternal One]. Sometimes they regard them subjectively, and speak of three stages of growth through which they pass, such as those of Beginner, Proficient and Perfect; or of phases of spiritual progress in which we first meditate upon reality, then contemplate reality, and at last we are united with reality.

If it is true, as I believe, that the phases of the NDE are both maps of heaven and states of consciousness, then some important conclusions can be made. Not only does the state of near-death consciousness differ from ordinary consciousness, near-death states differ from each other, deepening after each successive near-death phase. Consequently, even though many NDErs have momentarily achieved a high state of mystical consciousness, chances are that none has achieved perfection. They are becoming mystics, not going mad.

TABLE 1

Archaic Magic Mythic	Rational	Psychic Subtle Causal
Pre-Rational (Subconscious)	Rational Selfconscious	Trans-Rational (Superconscious)

(Ken Wilber, *Spiritual Choices*, p. 240)

TABLE 2

Near-Death Phases	Mystical Stages	Trans-Rational Levels
	Beginner Purgation	
1. Peace		
2. Out-of-Body	psychic	psychic
	Proficient Illumination	
3. World of Light	visionary	subtle
4. Being of Light		
5. Darkness/Void		
	Perfect Union	causal

Mystics and Metaphysics

A secular society requires proof that the mystic isn't mad. Proper proof can be provided by examining our basic assumptions about reality using the disciplines of philosophy and sociology. However, an intense emotional reaction to the NDE often precedes and feeds intellectual inquiry.

Emotional response to the NDE is seldom apathetic. People are usually either attracted or repelled. Negative reactions are expressed by the emotions of fear, anger, or envy. Indeed, intellectual skepticism may be a rationalization for a more instantaneous and primal emotional reaction to the challenge presented by the NDE to one's norms or world-view. The NDE presents the potential for shattering the structure of reality upon which one's life rests, however precariously. Fear and anger to such a threat is justified. The imminent destruction of a world-view is a kind of death.

Envy, on the other hand, is often prompted by the challenge presented to one's own spiritual supremacy or institutional prerogatives. Envy may, however, be a positive emotion, impelled by the divine desire arising in response to the near-death message. In these cases, the envious party seeks to emulate, rather than decapitate the NDEr.

The key issue here, as in the diagnosis of psychosis, is the question of the nature of reality, which is a philosophical or metaphysical question. I understand that many NDErs return with the need to redefine "normal." I returned with a need to redefine "reality." In that process, I rediscovered philosophy, especially epistemology, the sub-discipline of philosophy concerned with the question of knowledge — what we know and how we know it.

The principle mistake of near-death studies to date is, I believe, that both discoveries and the debate between what Zalesky calls "naive believers" and skeptics has been conducted within the framework of our culture's implicit and hence unconscious metaphysic — materialism. The word "materialism" denotes not only a consumer culture, but one which believes unerringly in matter as ultimate reality. This implicit metaphysic can be made conscious, and other philosophical possibilities presented that make better sense of the NDE.

Other viable philosophical options exist. In Hinduism and Buddhism, for instance, the metaphysical substructure is "idealism" in which mind or consciousness assumes ultimate reality. During my experience I made a similar discovery: that mind, not matter, was the ultimate building block of the universe. By mind, I do not mean the brain, or rational dualistic consciousness, but the existence of another dimension: higher consciousness, Christ-consciousness or Spirit, that is accessible to human intelligence and the source of Truth and inspiration.

Hindu philosophy is based on the information received during the meditative state. This information is accorded a higher place in the scale of human intelligence than the technical or rational reason we so admire in the West. In the West, the development of science and technology appeared to justify the conclusion that materialism was correct. The function of philosophy to discover Truth became obsolete, as science became the sole authority. God became a figment of human imagination. Under the challenge to accommodate the secular world, the liberal church has also become "materialistic." The Protestant theologian Paul Tillich has, for instance, defined God as "what matters to us ultimately."

In the midst of this materialistic gloom, there is one philosophical star, mathematician and philosopher Alfred North Whitehead. In *Process and Reality*, he constructs a philosophy that can explain both mystical experience and the reality of the average man or woman living in this world and in a scientific age. The potential of Whitehead's philosophy to explicate religious ideas in a scientific age has been developed by process theologians.

Reality, for Whitehead, is not static nor mechanical, but organismic; a process of the evolution of interrelated systems. Howard Storm tells me that Whitehead's view of reality corresponds to what he learned during his NDE.

God exists in Whitehead's system, but not as a "deus ex machina," a mechanic who set the clockwork world in motion and remains unmoved and impotent outside the system. God, for Whitehead, is the nature of both order and novelty. God works in the world, maintaining order and drawing the purposeful cosmos forward toward some final conclusion of the Good. While they are perhaps no more than an abstraction for Whitehead, Plato's realm of archetypes and ideas has been revitalized by him as the repository for the Good. Good is a co-creation of God and humans, in their capacity to appropriate and objectify the good of God.

Though Whitehead's philosophy has the obvious advantage of providing a metaphysical system which could unite theology and science, his most important contribution to a metaphysical understanding of the NDE is to be found in his epistemology. Whitehead calls his philosophy a modified idealism. Mind, or subject, once more becomes the basis for reality. Though Whitehead agrees that there is something out there which we can call objective reality, he doubts that we will ever be able to know what it is. The "symbol," an inextricable and unavoidable union of concept and percept is all we shall ever know. We are confined by the limits of our perceptual capacities and by the concepts, or ideas, or beliefs about reality which we hold in our minds.

Hence, according to Whitehead, Zalesky is essentially correct in calling the NDE a symbol or set of symbols. Symbols, however, form the basis of our human earthly experience also. We are no more likely to observe objective reality directly in this world than we are in the next. Whitehead's epistemology, therefore, reduces real distinctions between this world and the next, and potentially subjects them both to intellectual scrutiny.

Calling the NDE a symbol without providing a coherent metaphysic invites reductionisms. The current interest in symbolism is, however, more likely to make the world of the mystic and NDEr accessible to others. Mystics think in symbols, that is in words, ideas and images which convey multiple meanings simultaneously. Paradox and poetry become the "lingua franca" of the mystic, rather than the discursive, linear, dualistically logical style prevalent in our culture. Transcendence of rational thought and language during a NDE may feature in later communication difficulties.

An understanding of symbols can also facilitate an assessment of the spiritual and religious content of the heavenly journey. When God appears under form, the guise or veil is, by necessity, particular. That is, when NDErs see God, they view God in the particular form taken by their religious tradition. Since the God beyond form or image is Universal, NDErs whose experience is beyond images tend to be more universal in their religious response.

The discussion of philosophy and language may appear abstruse, but it is necessary to think about our language and experience in new ways in order to make room for new realities. Whitehead also felt it was necessary to think about experience. However, he also believed in common sense, as do NDErs. Their common sense tells them that what they experienced was real, more real than this world. To deny them their common sense reality is likely to create craziness.

Social Reality and Spiritual Community

Philosophy is not the only intellectual discipline concerned with the nature of reality. Sociologist Peter Berger has described the process by which all cultures create and define their reality: through common language, experience and concensus. Berger extends his sociological exploration of reality into the religious domain in two books, *The Sacred Canopy* and *Rumor of Angels*. In them he contends that theology has reneged on its function to represent the transcendent in culture and joined the mainstream majority. Theology should, he feels, remain a minority culture committed to discovering "rumours of angels" like these near-death stories.

In *The Social Construction of Reality*, co-authored with Luckmann, Berger describes how each culture defines its safe circle, or nomos, its norms for reality and behavior. He describes what happens to the deviate, the one who stands on the edge of the safe circle. Since the deviate reminds the inhabitants of the "safe circle" of their own mortality and capacity for insanity, they are scapegoated. Berger has here described the situation of the NDEr who, having returned from death and the experience of a new reality, threatens the comfort, safety and security of others.

Furthermore, Berger goes on to suggest that minority cultures shape themselves in the same fashion as the majority: through common experience, language and concensus. Thus the NDErs and the mystic together shape a common minority community based on a cohesive and coherent world-view that differs radically in many respects from the majority culture. The majority consider matter the ultimate reality, and unquestioningly accept the conclusions of their five senses. To the average American, the rational intellect or ego is the epitome of intellectual development, science is the accepted arbiter of truth, and God either doesn't exist or is a figment of imagination or creation of the human mind. Language is linear and limited to signs or words that have a single meaning. To them, objects have an ultimately reality "out there." Anything in the mind is merely subjective and less real.

On the other hand, the mystic has learned by experience that spiritual realities exist. For the mystic, the Divine, Spirit, or God is the Ultimate Reality, and this world a poor reflection. Mystics trust their supersenses. Mystics believe that Truth resides in the Mind of God, and that true information and inspiration flow from there, however distorted they may be by the human channel. Mystics understand the nature of both language and reality to be multidimensional, and they speak in metaphors, symbols and images. Communication is often telepathic, and community shaped on the common bond with God as well as each other. Through mutual experience and insight, they validate each other's world-view. The power of the near-death movement is, therefore, that it is providing an opportunity to create an alternative minority mystical community, which in turn can effectively challenge and change our counseling models, if not our world.

A minority mystical community created by consensus and validating its own norms is not mad, merely different. Consequently clinical models developed by and for the majority culture are inappropriate. Spiritual models meant for these mystics have been developed by transpersonal psychologists like Ken Wilber.

Chapter 7
Near-Death Recovery

Return to life is often as difficult as dying. The NDEr has changed dramatically and requires time, understanding and perhaps professional help to recover and return to full life. The temporary imbalance and confusion is not caused by deterioration, but rapid and profound growth. The old self — morals, mores, mental attitudes, etc. — have dissolved, but the newborn self is still unformed. It took Barbara Harris seven years to become the real self she had glimpsed during her NDE. Recovery time may be longer for those who have had deep NDEs, whose families are unsympathetic, or whose emotional and mental maturity was underdeveloped prior to the NDE.

Recovery needs range from career changes and marriage problems, to self concerns such as continued personal and spiritual growth along the path suggested in the NDE, and confusion about the profound and startling spiritual changes. Some simply need a sympathetic ear in order to understand and integrate the experience.

Change alone is hard. The spiritual changes undergone during a NDE present a special challenge both to the NDEr and their families. Information about mystical experience is scarce in our society. Materialism is the norm. According to those norms, the NDEr may appear crazy. That label and even diagnosis is the largest problem many NDErs face. It retards recovery and limits access to much needed professional help.

Social alienation is only one-half of the recovery equation. Spiritual changes may be personally unsettling to the experiencer. Sudden acquisition of psychic senses and information, new energy, new emotional expression, inexplicable depression, increased sensitivity and so forth may require special care. It is these spiritual side-effects which are confused with psychotic symptoms and seeking a transpersonal therapist or competent spiritual guide could be helpful.

NDErs often do not seek professional help even when needed, legitimately fearing a diagnosis of psychosis. English professor Martha Todd related to Raymond Moody what happened after her NDE. Her doctor

"...told my parents that I was delirious and hallucinating. He wanted me to see a psychiatrist right away. They thought I had lost my mind and

I was sent to a mental hospital for treatment. I just couldn't believe that this was happening to me."

NDErs need to exercise caution in choosing a therapist. They should seek someone who understands and respects their experience. I chose a therapist who had had a NDE in childhood in addition to a Ph.D. in clinical psychology. I believe shared experience is as important as clinical knowledge, since subtle differences can arise between client and therapist which may retard therapy.

Counselors who encounter NDErs in their practice need to set aside some basic assumptions, or refer the NDErs to someone else. They need to have understanding about and respect for mystical experience, and be able to distinguish between psychotic symptoms and spiritual side-effects. They will need, I feel, to readjust the concept of the self to include a soul or spirit, and understand the potential for human growth beyond the rational ego. They will not insist the NDEr readjust to pre-existing social norms, but help them in the struggle to rearrange their lives around the new and higher norms envisioned in the experience. Above all, therapists will have to test their tolerance for difference, for unrepressed emotional expression, and be prepared to change if they accept a NDEr as a client.

Listening

There is, however, something that even sympathetic family and friends can do to help the NDErs. They can listen. "Finding someone who will listen is the most significant and often the most frustrating initial problem near-death experiencers encounter after their experiences. They are rebuffed for many reasons, such as suspicions of insanity, envy and fear." Failure to speak of the experience can precipitate clinical depression.

The following guidelines for listening, developed by a NDEr and social worker, are presented in some detail. They could form a miniature guidebook for near-death care, as they address some of the specific concerns of these people. I have underlined those sentences which I feel deserve particular attention.

1. A near-death experiencer needs someone to listen. Though it may sound simple, many near-death experiencers find that others either <u>dismiss their stories, interpret them in terms of existing theories, or refuse to listen in a genuinely respectful way.</u>
2. Listeners should realize that near-death experiencers are initially somewhat <u>uneasy</u> about sharing accounts of their experiences. The experiencer should therefore be assured of <u>confidentiality.</u>
3. Because experiencers are often anxious about what others may be thinking about them, listeners should be assured that having had an <u>experi-</u>

ence is fairly common and is not evidence of mental instability. This should not, however, be done in such a way as to trivialize the experience, such as saying, "oh, that's nothing; that happens all the time."

4. Listeners should not treat the experience as something that will "just go away." Such an approach is futile . . .

5. Once trust and rapport have been established, listeners should avoid imposing their own interpretations of the experience. Trying to analyze the experience inhibits near-death experiencers. It is important to remember that no matter how bizarre it may sound, the experience is the most significant, profound thing that has ever happened to most near-death experiencers, and near-death experiencers may display considerable emotion.

6. Despite the overwhelming positive nature of the near-death experience, many near-death experiencers express anger and frustration at the rejection they have met and at having been unable to integrate the experience fully into their lives. In this regard, it is helpful for near-death experiencers to have other experiencers to talk with, because only other near-death experiencers can fully comprehend and share the profound depths of the experience.

Individual Counseling

Professional help may be desirable beyond the step of simple listening. The counselor who elects to become an NDE care giver will find it a rewarding, though at times trying relationship. They will encounter people who feel they have had the most wonderful experience of their life. Many will be in the midst of profound and rapid personal growth. Others may be initially confused, depressed or excessively emotional. They may encounter individuals with real conflicts over career or marriage as a result of personal change. Others may speak of their psychic or mystical experiences. The NDEr who enters a counselor's office may be initially "revved up" by the tremendous impact of new energy, insight, information, and capacity for feeling initiated by the NDE. Additionally, many may be undergoing conflicts at home and on the job, as a result of the rapid change in values and priorities and world view. These people need a safe place to discharge. With that in mind, I want to describe from my own experience and observation what you, the counselor, is likely to encounter and some simple, but effective, interventions.

The NDErs needs to talk excessively, so be prepared. Know your own tolerance for careful listening and apportion your available calendar hours accordingly. If you can only spare one hour a week, talking and listening can extend into months. If you can spare more time initially, that would be helpful.

The tremendous need to talk has its origins in several aspects of the NDE. The energy absorbed during the NDE, particularly the encounter with the Light, needs to be discharged. Talking is one method of discharge.

The timelessness of the NDE means that a lot happened in a very short period of earth time. As an example recall that an entire life-review can occur in a matter of minutes. To tell the whole story may take considerable time. If the totality of the experience is to be understood and integrated, the entire experience needs to be remembered and recounted.

The act of speaking accelerates integration by objectifying the experience. It is as if by hearing one's own words, or seeing them on paper, one is given a new, more objective perspective. Understanding of the experience, and incorporation into the totality of the psyche, takes place more rapidly under these conditions.

Having someone to listen is important, for it helps the individual to return to the human community. Active listening of the sort that offers confirming, clarifying or inquiring feed-back would be more helpful still. Finally, there seems to be a need on the part of the NDErs to tell and retell their story that is similar to those in mourning. Perhaps the repetitive retelling of any crisis event is an intrinsic part of the healing process.

In addition to excessive talking, these people may present themselves as confused, excessively emotional, or with what may appear to be inappropriate behavior. Any of these responses are sensible when viewed in the context of the experience. They are not necessarily pathological, but may require care.

A psychiatrist's assistant has described the NDErs they have seen in their office as initially "very confused and depressed. They believe they have had a nervous breakdown." Explaining that they have had a NDE or related spiritual experience may dispel some of the initial confusion. The impact of such rapid and total change should be expected to cause confusion. Time is needed to ask questions and to sort it out. Much of the initial apparent confusion may be a result of a sudden change in both the way of thinking and a rapid influx of new information and ideas. These changes in cognition, coupled with the inevitable ineffability, may combine to present a confused state. Patience is needed and probing questions such as, "Can you tell me how you are thinking?," "Explain to me some of these new ideas, insights, information," "Can you find other words to describe the same event?" Assurance that these new ideas and thought processes are a normal concomitant of mystical experience may be helpful. Premature closure is not advisable for either counselor or NDEr. It may take a long time to discover the meaning of the experience.

As the NDE appears to expand consciousness, it unblocks the emotions as well. One woman said to me, "I had never felt emotion before in my life." This was related in the context of a group setting in which some of us wept exuberantly as we recalled earlier trauma and feelings, and as we relived our own deaths. The rest of the group had difficulty handling our emotional expression. It has been my experience that this is universally true. Society is emotionally repressed by NDE standards. The counselor will need to understand his or her own tolerance for emotional expression; and not expect the emotional deluge to be entirely positive. In addition to excessive weeping there may be a great deal of anger at loss of the light and at the treatement by others, past and present. I believe that if the counselor can provide a safe place to discharge the emotional excess, in time the NDEr will be able to accommodate his-her emotional expression to the needs and tolerance of the larger society.

The excess energy, together with the release of socialized and conventional patterns of behavior, results in a new spontaneity which may appear inappropriate. The often new and startling discovery that they are acceptable and that they have a right to think and feel for themselves may change previously excessively socialized, "good" individuals into assertive people. I believe these changes need to be encouraged, together with consideration for others. The counselor can provide a safe place to try out new behavior.

Beyond listening, the counselor can facilitate the sorting of mental confusion, the discharge of emotion and the experimentation with new behaviors. The next step in the process of the NDEr's recovery will be to aid in the clarification of new values, goals and priorities which result from insights received during the NDE. The decision to divorce or change careers may accompany this clarification.

The search for purpose could include vocational guidance. NDErs should be encouraged to choose and enter a helping profession to provide an outlet for the messianic zeal which often accompanies an NDE.

Marriage and Family Therapy

The emergence of marital conflict represents a real NDE concern, and the counselor may wish to refer or conduct sessions of family therapy. Anecdotal evidence suggests that the NDE population is marked by a high divorce rate. Most near-death marital problems can be attributed to the changes which accompany a NDE. A brief discussion of the outstanding areas of marital difficulty will be offered below. These are indicative of the problems of reentry into all social systems.

Families of returned NDErs are under stress. The emotional tension of near catastrophe and the convalescence of the NDEr must strain family resources. The aborted grief and desire to return to normal of the spouse conflict with the changes in the NDEr and his grief at needing to return to earth. The crisis may cause family problems to surface.

Barbara Harris did not tell her husband for two years.

> She said she didn't want me to think she was weird, her husband said.
> I don't really even know if she had an experience. She read about near-

death and suddenly decided she had one. Maybe she talked herself into believing she had one.

Barb's failure to communicate her NDE and her husband's discounting remark suggest the couple previously had trouble communicating. They can be compared to the good communication of Joe Geraci and his wife Joan, who are still married. Joe finally told Joan about his experiences about six months after it occurred.

> I was going to explode if I didn't tell anyone, he said. At first I kept it to myself because it was too personal. But Joan was an excellent listener and accepted what I had gone through. Talking to her made me feel much better.

The changes of the NDEr can be characterized as changes in perception, cognition, emotion, values, goals and world view. These result in new rules (what is right and what is real), new roles, new loyalties, etc., which may conflict with pre-NDE family standards. Education concerning the general near-death changes, together with a mutual tolerance of difference, would prove helpful.

Changes in values from material success to service and compassion create problems for spouses. The breadwinner may give up his job or change to a less lucrative position. Housewives and mothers may redefine their roles. As one of my respondents related: "They were no longer my God, nor was I theirs. There was some sadness in that." As service becomes a predominant motive, housewives may move into the professional sector. Barbara Harris' husband complained that rather than take care of the family, her mission was now to save the world. To achieve a new family balance, obligations to both self and family will have to be considered by both spouses.

The unconditional love of the Light has changed the NDErs idea of love. As Greyson has pointed out, "I love everyone" is difficult for their partners to understand. The spouse still believes in the love of dependency and jealousy. It may be necessary for the NDEr to relearn a more personalized form of love for their families, as Atwater suggests, as well as spouses to learn unconditional love.

All of the above changes present a significant impact on family balance. The counselor will aid the couple in determining whether a continuation of the marriage would enhance the well-being of both spouses. Assessment of the family around issues of flexibility, response to change, boundaries, enmeshment, communication and rules will enable the care-giver to design interventions appropriate to the family. The NDEr has changed, but is not perfect. Enough pre-NDE residue will remain to enable the astute clinician to find the problematic patterns and to change them. The NDEr has returned to the old family unit as new person, however. If the spouses elect to remain married both will grow, and the family unit will find a new balance.

I have seen at least two couples with extreme problems consisting of alcoholism, abuse and incest become more functional following a NDE. One of my respondents explained that she felt that her NDE was a break in the vicious family patterns of incest and alcohol so "the sins of the fathers would not be visited upon the children."

In summary, the marriage counselor will encounter a changed person returned to family units of varying degrees of healthy functioning. While the prognosis of previously dysfunctional families may be poor, the NDE crisis may provide the "transformative leap" necessary to move the family from dysfunction to relative health.

Counselors may also wish to refer the NDEr to the local Friends of IANDS (International Association for Near-Death Studies) support group, and are encouraged, themselves, to attend.

Friends of IANDS

The perceived need for NDErs to gather together resulted in the formation of a national support group, Friends of IANDS. Martha Fortune, a registered nurse and former instructor in the School of Nursing of the University of Rochester, NDEr Tom Sawyer and I formed the Rochester, New York near-death support group in December of 1988. Psychiatrist Dr. Fred Remington acted as consultant to our coordinating team. Each month we issued a press release to the local media inviting NDErs, those who have had other mystical experiences, and interested professionals to attend. Response was favorable. NDErs, those who have had other mystical experiences, interested professionals, and spiritual seekers attended meetings. There was a core group of about eleven.

Presented below are my impressions of experiencer needs which are met by this support group. Some of the reasons given for attendance have been: "I need this group. Without you I feel totally alone." This person's world view had changed dramatically and rapidly to a mystical one. She needed the group for personal validation.

"I need this group. It is the only place I have to discuss the marital conflicts that have developed as a result of my experience," said another group member. Marital conflicts are a popular topic. Despite the high divorce rate among NDErs, all of us remain married. We share the same conflicts and can share strategies, with spouses attending as well. Our discussions have breathed life into textbook cases.

"You are not the same person I married" is a classic comment. One spouse exclaimed, "I brought one person to the hospital and took another one home."

Anger and grief are common responses by spouses to such rapid change, though entire families may react in similar fashion. The children of another woman complained that even though she was nicer, they missed their old mother. Even positive change requires readjustment.

In addition to the rapid personality changes, the NDEr is seeing things invisible to the spouse, or having inexplicable or extreme emotional reactions. Recently a woman recounted in group what had happened to her as her mother-in-law was dying. The mother-in-law came to her, in spirit, during meditation to tell her that she was ready to go and was about to die. The woman told her mother-in-law not to go now, that everyone had to be there when she died. They arranged for a suitable time. The mother-in-law died, and the NDEr saw her spirit dancing with joy above the dead body. Her spouse listened to this story with rapt attention, unusual for an NDEr's spouse, who often assume the NDEr is crazy. The support group can, however, listen with calm and great interest. Most of us have had similar experiences. As one woman said, "I need this group. It is the only place where I can talk openly about my spiritual experiences."

Some of us have shared experiences we haven't and wouldn't share with anyone else. For others, it may be the first time they have shared their NDE. We understand how difficult it is, and are supportive. We can tolerate the tears.

In summary, the IANDS support group facilitates talking, allows the individual validation for their world view, provides opportunity to discuss ongoing marital issues and a safe place to share spiritual experiences. Spouses who attend are often helped by realizing neither they nor the spouse is alone.

Spiritual Side effects

In addition to marital and career problems, search for self, meaning and purpose, and new growth which NDErs have in common with everyone, they suffer from a set of side effects peculiar to mystics. These side effects may precipitate a spiritual crisis, a term coined by Stanislav and Christina Grof for sudden spiritual change which has gotten temporarily out of control, and may require trained transpersonal or spiritual, rather than psychiatric, care. At least four near-death aftereffects may result in spiritual crisis: sudden psychic opening, inflation, depression and sudden energy arousal.

Sudden Psychic Opening. The sudden acquisition of psychic abilities following a near-death experience can be disturbing or devastating. Georgia, who was quoted in Chapter 5, continued to have psychic abilities, but she learned to control and integrate them into her normal life. Cliff was not so fortunate. According to Ring his prophetic visions caused him to suffer a nervous breakdown. Information concerning global catastrophe can itself be catastrophic.

Treatment may include learning conscious control, or ignoring the "mental noise." In time it will dissipate.

In many spiritual-mystical traditions, psychic abilities are an expected aspect of early spiritual awakening. Certain Buddhist and Hindu texts enumerate the various supernormal powers and issue warning to the serious spiritual aspirant that these are "stumbling blocks on the path to truth (and) . . . obstacles to same." Christian mystics also utter warnings concerning the potential abuses of the same supernormal powers. They can prevent the mystic from achieving the goal of God union. They can be misused and they can be the occasion of dangerous psychic inflation, but they usually cannot be avoided.

Psychic abilities, then, are an expected concommitant of spiritual mystical awakenings. They are signs that wakening from natural to supernatural vision has occurred. The experiencer has a choice concerning these new abilities. They may be suppressed in pursuit of either normal waking consciousness or further spiritual growth. Or they may be cultivated as an expression of either human or transpersonal potential. If the latter course is chosen, the experiencer needs to exercise caution. These gifts always contain the potential for abuse and for inflation.

Inflation (blown up, distended with air, unrealistically large and important; hence to be vain, pompous, proud, presumptuous). I have witnessed several examples of near-death inflation. However, these are unlikely to be reported by the experiencer as aftereffects which require care. Evidence is most likely to come from the spouse, or others intimate with the experiencer.

"Ego's taking credit for transpersonal [spiritual] faculties is at the heart of transpersonal inflation," according to transpersonal psychologist Gary Rosenthal. The theoretical understanding and treatment of spiritual inflation therefore differs from ordinary inflation. Spiritual and transpersonal theory recognizes the reality of the gifts but assigns them to the Source of all life rather than the personal ego. Treatment consists of separating the Source and the ego. Disconfirming feedback can be given to the experiencer, but not the experience. I have found the practice of divine Thanksgiving and the practice of humility as outlined by St. Theresa of Avila to be helpful in combatting personal inflation.

Prolonged inflation contains the potential for psychosis, according to Grey. Inflation is also contagious. Counselors and others who encounter NDErs should refrain from placing them on a pedestal. They are not perfected saints.

Depression. Cycles of depression alternate with elevated moods due either to inflation or to honest spiritual elevation. Depression may be an intrinsic part of the spiritual process, or caused by poor clinical treatment. It may be precipitated by inhibiting growth to the new transcendent level of self, either through drugs, devaluation or silencing. Bette Furn says in the *Journal of Near Death Studies* that:

Sorrow, anguish and the inability for many to be able to successfully communicate to others the profundity of what has occurred, often may signal the beginning of a major clinical depression. (It is important to note that the depression as expressed by the NDEr will differ in some significant ways from the more typical case, in terms of diagnostic criteria...for example, feelings of worthlessness, excessive guilt and suicidal ideation are highly unlikely. The affective pain, however, is intense.)

The following anecdotal account of one woman whom Ring met, illustrates a severe clinical depression which resulted when the NDE was suppressed. While still in the hospital, she tried three times to tell her story. Each time she was told to be quiet. The third person told her she was crazy, and she stopped trying to share. Ten years later, at a lecture by Ring, she was given an opportunity to share her experience. The clinical depression lifted immediately as attested to by her psychiatrist.

Depression may also be an intrinsic part of the spiritual process, a dark night of the soul as Wilber calls it, in *Transformations of Consciousness*.

Once the soul obtains a direct experience of the Divine, with concomitant vision, ecstasy, or clarity, and that experience begins to fade (which it initially does) the soul may suffer a profound abandonment depression (not to be confused with borderline neurotic or existential depression). In this case, the soul has seen its meaning in life, its daemon or destiny, only to have it fade — that is the Dark Night — It may be noted that no matter how profound the depression or agony of the Dark night might be, the literature contains no cases of its leading to suicide.

Joe Geraci told Ring about his grief at loss of the Light.

It was at least, at least, six months after the incident that I, that I could even speak to my wife about it. It was such an emotional, beautiful, swelling feeling inside that every time I tried to express it, I think I would just explode, you know; I would break down and cry. And she, for the longest time couldn't figure out what was wrong with me...

[In the hospital, immediately upon regaining consciousness, he recalls] I remember being very angry that they brought me back and my wife ended up asking me why, later. "You seemed angry, how come?" I just couldn't tell her...

That was probably the most frustrating six months of my existence. After experiencing perfection and something so beautiful, I wanted to hold onto it. I didn't want to let go. And it wasn't easy.

Joe had an exceptional pastor who accepted Joe's experience, and enabled him to consequently accept return to life. He reminded Joe that the Light would be there for him when he returned. I believe for many NDErs, however, entrance into a spiritual path would provide techniques for recovering the Light as much as is possible in this life. Total renunciation isn't necessary. Wilber also suggests reading in the mystical literature and petitionary prayer as methods for overcoming spiritual depression.

Energy Arousal. Unusual energy arousal, called Kundalini by researchers, has been noted following an NDE. Two transpersonal treatment modalies are recommended. The individual must either "ride it out" or take up a contemplative discipline. These unusual energy experiences are often treated with drugs by a conventional psychiatrist. This stops the course of spiritual growth, and should be avoided.

Spiritual Side-Effects and Psychotic Symptoms

There are two definitions of insanity operating against the NDEr — the clinical and the cultural. The NDEr usually suffers from cultural rather than clinical stereotypes. Any deviance from social norms, particularly our culture's materialistic assumptions, will be viewed as insanity. Throughout the book, but particularly in the chapter on mysticism, I have challenged those assumptions. I have stated that while the mystic may differ from the average individual, he or she belongs to a legitimate mystical community which establishes its own norms.

Unfortunately cultural biases often affect clinical judgments as well. In fact, many of the presuppositions concerning mental illness have arisen in a materialistic context, and

> In such a context, were a person not only to believe in the reality of God, but also have an experience of God . . . then such a person would be demonstrating an "impairment of reality testing" — which is "a priori," a definition of psychosis . . . [There are no such things as] "transpersonal disturbances" in Chagrin Falls, Ohio! For there (or in turn-of-the-century Vienna) one is simply presumed crazy.

Even the mystically informed therapist, however, may have difficulty discerning spiritual side-effects from psychotic symptoms. Though I spent a year as a pastoral counselor under supervision at the Rochester Psychiatric Center and two years as co-facilitator of a near-death support group, I have difficulty describing those differences to those who have not had mystical experience.

I believe it is important to have intimate knowledge of both psychotics and NDErs before such discrimination is possible. Since acquiring that expertise, I also find glorification of schizophrenia as false as the reduction of mystical states to mental illness. Mental illness is a real and terrible condition, not to be confused with mysticism. Psychotics and mystics are two distinct groups who may superficially appear similar but are deeply different. Perhaps the greatest difference is qualitative. The NDEr may be characterized by such positive qualities as joy, energy, love, service, growth, and so forth.

A sympathetic understanding of the NDE and mysticism is also a necessary prelude to the distinction between spiritual side-effects and psychotic symptoms. Without the understanding that for twelve million NDErs and many more mystics these experiences are normal, there can be no differentiation. I believe it is this initial, incredulous response to the mystical visions of the NDE that result in immediate psychiatric hospitalization. In our society a mystic vision is *ipso facto* an hallucination.

There is, however, a difference. Psychotics hallucinate. Mystics have visions. Visions are based on spiritual realities. The mystic or NDEr is seeing or hearing something that is really there. To test this, ask another mystic, or compare the vision, apparition, or inspiration to those recorded in the psychic, spiritual and mystical literature.

Mystical visions are usually positive and often divine. The psychotics whom I have met generally prefer the FBI and the CIA. Unike psychotics, mystics share their experiences in community. Not only do they have similar experiences while alone, they are capable of communal viewing. They actively seek others like themselves and so, unlike psychotics, are capable of forming community.

There are other spiritual side-effects which mimic psychotic symptoms besides visions. Spiritually natural mood and energy cycles have been misdiagnosed as manic-depression. The normal near-death desire to die is confused with suicidal tendencies, and the unrepressed emotional state diagnosed as pathological rather than the result of natural spiritual expansion. Near-death loss of boundaries indicate personality disorder to the clinician rather than the high state of mystical unitive consciousness that it is. Dissociative states may be inferred from the superreal sense, memory loss and new identity that normally accompany mystical states as well as the NDE. And poetic and symbolic utterance can be mistaken for psychobabble. Unlike the psychotic's metaphoric garbage, near-death symbols will eventually make sense.

According to Atwater, NDErs may remain permanently paranoid, probably due to their constant persecution, or stay space cadets. The spaciness of the NDEr may go undetected by the clinician, but will be apparent to a good spiritual teacher. The ecstatic flight of the NDE has resulted in a loss of earthly roots. NDErs often need to learn how to "ground" as it is called in the spiritual traditions. Acceptance of life and discovery of purpose result in well-grounded NDErs, who are at home in this world as well as the next.

I believe that continued spiritual growth should be as much a part of near-death recovery as counseling. The spiritual traditions of the world's religions have provided techniques for ecstatic flight and regrounding. Entrance onto a spiritual path would provide the teaching and techniques by which NDErs could overcome some of the more debilitating side-effects. There they would receive validation for their experience and world-view and incentive to take the initiatory experience of the NDE on to higher and more sustained levels of spiritual consciousness.

Not all NDErs may want to continue spiritual growth. They may be content to return and remain an integral member of the ordinary world. However, once implanted, the spiritual vision and divine desire may be hard to uproot. Following a spiritual path provides the means of maintaining the mystical vision in the midst of life. It also provides a way for those who have not yet tasted the NDE to begin their own spiritual discovery.

Recovery is complete when the initial confusion and disorientation has dissipated, when new gifts have been understood and assimilated and when the NDEr's life and self have been re-integrated and re-organized around the new center discovered in the experience. Re-creation, or the continual emergence of new human and spiritual stages, is never completed.

Selected Bibliography

Anthony, D.; B. Ecker; and K. Wilber, ed. *Spiritual Choices: The Problem of Recognizing Authentic Paths to InnerTransformation.* New York: Paragon House, 1987.

Atwater, P.M.H. *Coming Back to Life: The After-Effects of the Near-Death Experience.* New York: Ballantine Books, 1988.

————. "The Seven Most Common After Effects of Survival: The Inability to Personalize Emotions." *Vital Signs,* vol. 3, no. 3 (December 1983), pp. 12-13.

————. "The Seven Most Common After Effects of Survival: The Inability to Recognize and Comprehend Boundaries, Rules, Limits." *Vital Signs,* vol. 3, no. 4 (Spring 1984), p. 14.

————. "The Seven Most Common After Effects of Survival: IV Expanded/ Enhanced Sensibilities — Becoming More Intuitive, Knowing, Spatial, Non-linear in Perceptions, a Sense of Timelessness." *Vital Signs,* vol. 4, no. 3 (Winter 1984-85), pp. 14-15.

————. "Surviving the Near-Death Experience." *New Realities,* vol. 9, no. 3 (January-February 1989), pp. 14-19, 48-51.

Berger, Peter. *A Rumor of Angels: Modern Society and the Rediscovery of the Supernatural.* Garden City: Doubleday, 1969.

Berger, Peter. *Sacred Canopy: Elements of a Sociological Theory of Religion.* Garden City: Doubleday, 1967.

Berger, Peter, and Luckmann, Thomas. *Social Construction of Reality: A Treatise in Sociology of Knowledge.* Garden City: Doubleday, 1966.

Clark, Kimberly. "Response to Adjustment and the Near Death Experience." Journal of Near Death Studies, vol. 6, no. 1 (Fall 1987), pp. 20-23.

Eckhart, Meister. *The Essential Sermons, Commentaries, and Defense of Meister Eckhart.* Translation and introduction by Edmund Colledge and Bernard McGinn, preface by Huston Smith. New York: Paulist Press, 1981.

Flynn, Charles P. *After the Beyond.* Englewood Cliffs, New Jersey: Prentice-Hall, Inc., 1986.

Furn, Bette G. "Adjustment and the Near-Death Experience; A Conceptual and Therapeutic Model." *Journal of Near Death Studies,* vol. 6, no. 1 (Fall 1987), pp. 4-19.

Gallup, George, Jr., with Proctor, William. *Adventures in Immortality.* New York: McGraw-Hill Book Co., 1982.

Geraci, Joseph. "Comments on Bette Furn's Adjustment and the Near-Death Experience." *Journal of Near-Death Studies,* vol. 6, no. 1 (Fall 1987), pp. 28-29.

Grey, Margot. *Return from Death.* London: Arkana, 1985.

Greyson, Bruce. "Near-Death Experiences and Attempted Suicide," *Suicide and Life-Threatening Behavior,* vol. 11, no. 1 (Spring 1981), pp. 10-16.

———. "A Typology of Near-Death Experiences." *The American Journal of Psychiatry,* vol. 140, no. 8 (May 1983), pp. 967-969.

———. "The Near-Death Experience Scale: Construction, Reliability, and Validity." *The Journal of Nervous and Mental Disease,* vol. 171, no. 6 (1983), pp. 369-375.

———. "Near-Death Experiences and Personal Values." *The American Journal of Psychiatry,* vol. 142, no. 8 (August 1985), pp. 618-628.

———. "Incidence of Near-Death Experiences Following Attempted Suicide." *Suicide and Life-Threatening Behavior,* vol. 16, no. 1 (1986), pp. 40-45.

Greyson, Bruce, and Stevenson, Ian. "The Phenomenology of Near-Death Experiences." *Journal of Psychiatry,* vol. 137, no. 10 (October 1980), pp. 1193-1196.

Greyson, Bruce, and Harris, Barbara. "Clinical Approaches to the Near Death Experiencer." *Journal of Near-Death Studies,* vol. 6, no. 1 (Fall 1987), pp. 41-52.

Grof, Stanislav, ed. *Ancient Wisdom and Modern Science.* Albany: State University of New York Press, 1984.

Grof, Stanislav. *Beyond the Brain.* Albany: State University of New York Press, 1985.

Grof, Stanislav, and Grof, Christina. *Beyond Death: The Gates of Consciousness.* London: Thames and Hudson, 1980.

Grof, Christina, and Grof, Stanislav. "Spiritual Emergency: Understanding and Treatment of Transpersonal Crises, Part I." *Vital Signs,* vol. 5, no. 1 (Summer 1985), pp. 1-7.

Grosso, Michael. *The Final Choice.* Walpole, New Hampshire: Stillpoint Publishing, 1985.

Hampe, Johann C. *To Die Is Gain.* Translated by Margaret Kohl. London: Darton, Longman & Todd, 1979.

Hoffman, Lynn. *Foundations of Family Therapy.* New York: Basic Books, 1981.

Huxley, Aldous. *The Perennial Philosophy.* New York: Harper & Bros., 1945.

James, William. *The Varieties of Religious Experience.* New York: Random House, 1902.

Krishna, Gopi. *Kundalini*. Boston: Shambhala, 1971.

Langer, Suzzanne K. *Philosophy in a New Key*. Cambridge: Harvard University Press, 1957.

Lee, Anthony. "The Lazarus Syndrome." *RN*, vol. 41, no. 1 (June 1978), pp. 54-64.

Maslow, Abraham H. *Towards a New Psychology of Being*. 2nd ed. New York: D. Van Nostrand Co., 1968.

McDonagh, John. "Review of Bette Furn's Adjustment and the Near-Death Experience." *Journal of Near-Death Studies*, vol. 6, no. 1 (Fall 1987), pp. 24-27.

Moody, Raymond A. *Life After Life*. Covington, Georgia: Mockingbird Books, Bantam Books, 1976.

———. *Reflections on Life After Life*. Covington, Georgia: Mockingbird Books, Bantam Books, 1977.

———. *The Light Beyond*. New York: Bantam Books, 1988.

Olson, Melodie. "The Incidence of Out-of-Body Experiences in Hospitalized Patients." *Journal of Near-Death Studies*, vol. 6, no. 3 (Spring 1988), pp. 169-174.

Osis, Karlis, and Haraldsson, Erlendur. *At the Hour of Death*. New York: Avon Books, 1977.

Petroff, Elizabeth A. *Medieval Women's Visionary Literature*. Oxford: Oxford University Press, 1986.

Ring, Kenneth. *Life at Death*. New York: Quill, 1982.

———. *Heading Toward Omega*. New York: Wm. Morrow, 1984.

Roberts, Bernadette. *The Path To No-Self*. Boston & London: Shambhala, 1985.

Sabom, Michael B. *Recollections of Death*. New York: Harper & Row, 1982.

St. John of the Cross. *The Collected Works of St. John of the Cross*. Translated by Kiernan Kavanaugh and Otilio Rodriquez. Washington, D.C.: ICS Publication, 1979.

———. *Selected Writings of St. John of the Cross*. Kiernan Kavanaugh, editor. New York: Paulist Press, 1987.

St. Theresa of Avila. *The Life of Theresa of Jesus*. E. Allison Peers, translator and editor. Garden City, New York: Image Books, Doubleday and Co. Inc., 1960.

———. *Interior Castle of St. Theresa of Avila*. Translated by Allison E. Peers. Garden City: Doubleday, 1961.

Steinbuch, Yaron A. "Near-Death Experiences: The After Effects." 1986. Unpublished Manuscript.

Szarmach, Paul E. *An Introduction to the Medieval Mystics of Europe*. Albany: State University of New York Press, 1984.

Tart, Charles T., ed. *Transpersonal Psychologies*. California: Psychological Processes, Inc., 1983.

Tillich, Paul. *Systematic Theology* 3 vols. Chicago: University of Chicago Press, 1951-1963.

Underhill, Evelyn. *Mysticism.* 10th ed. London: Methuen and Co. Ltd., 1923.

Whitehead, Alfred North. *Process and Reality.* London: Collier Macmillan Publ., 1929.

———. *Symbolism.* New York: Macmillan Co., 1958.

Wilber, Ken. *The Spectrum of Consciousness.* Wheaton, Illinois: The Theosophical Publishing House, 1977.

———. *Atman Project.* Wheaton Illinois: Theosophical Publishing House, 1980.

———. *No Boundary: Eastern and Western Approaches to Personal Growth.* Shambhala, 1981.

Wilber, Ken; Engler, Jack; and Brown, Daniel P. *Transformations of Consciousness: Conventional and Contemplative Perspectives on Development.* Boston & London: Shambhala, 1986.

Woods, Richard, ed. *Understanding Mysticism.* Garden City, New York: Doubleday and Company, 1980.

Zalesky, Carol. *Otherworld Journeys: Accounts of Near-Death Experience in Medieval and Modern Times.* New York, Oxford: Oxford University Press, 1987.